TOO BUSY FOR LOVE

PHOEBE MACLEOD

Boldwood

First published in Great Britain in 2024 by Boldwood Books Ltd.

Cover Design by Head Design Ltd

Cover Photography: Shutterstock

A CIP catalogue record for this book is available from the British Library.

Paperback ISBN 978-1-83533-342-6

Large Print ISBN 978-1-83533-338-9

Hardback ISBN 978-1-83533-337-2

Ebook ISBN 978-1-83533-335-8

Kindle ISBN 978-1-83533-336-5

Audio CD ISBN 978-1-83533-343-3

MP3 CD ISBN 978-1-83533-340-2

Digital audio download ISBN 978-1-83533-334-1

Boldwood Books Ltd
23 Bowerdean Street
London SW6 3TN
www.boldwoodbooks.com

To Mark. Thank you for being a better friend than I've often deserved.

1

If you'd asked me where I'd spend the evening of my twenty-ninth birthday, the last place I'd have said would have been a police holding cell. Yet this is where I am, and I still don't really understand how I ended up here.

The day started normally enough. My alarm went off just after five so I could shower and dress before going downstairs to supervise the breakfast service and guest checkout. I'm the manager of a small boutique hotel in Shoreditch, and every day starts pretty much the same way. Madame Dufour, the owner of the hotel, is a stickler for protocol and she relies on me to ensure standards don't drop. For example, although our restaurant doesn't open for lunch, she insists on full silver service for both breakfast and dinner. Our guests must be addressed by name wherever possible, to ensure they feel valued. I had to remind Amber on reception only this morning, when she failed to read the name on a guest's credit card and addressed him as 'sir'.

This morning. It feels like a lifetime ago as I cast my eyes around the bare, tiled cell. The mattress I'm sitting on is hopelessly thin and provides very little cushioning from the concrete slab that is allegedly the bed. I hope I don't end up being kept in here overnight; there's no way I'd be able to sleep on this. I wonder how Madame is coping. The cold concrete is going to be playing havoc with her rheumatoid arthritis.

My thoughts are interrupted by a commotion outside. It sounds like the guy is either drunk, high or both as he's shouting at the top of his voice and his speech is slurred.

'Don't you touch me, pig,' he yells. 'Do not put your hands on me, OK?'

'If you behave and go into the cell without a fight, nobody's going to touch you, Gary,' a calm voice replies. 'You know how this goes.'

Gary may know how this goes, but he's obviously decided not to behave, as I can clearly hear the sounds of a scuffle, along with Gary's voice shouting, 'Get off me, you bastards!' A cell door slams and Gary's protests are silenced.

I wonder if this is what an out-of-body experience is like. Your imagination takes you somewhere so completely unfamiliar that you just can't connect it to reality. That's kind of how I feel at the moment. My eyes are telling me very clearly that I'm in a police cell, but my brain is refusing to engage with it. I gaze around the small room once more and my eyes alight on the toilet in the corner. Now I come to think of it, I would quite like a wee, but I'm very conscious of the CCTV camera on the ceiling. There's nothing like the feeling that some big, burly guy is watching to make your bladder shy.

Things were fairly quiet when Madame called me into the hotel dining room just after three this afternoon. Our clientele is mainly overstressed City workers, so we offer a siesta service where they can check in at midday for a snooze, and we wake them at four so they can go back to their offices refreshed and ready to pull yet another all-nighter. Housekeeping then have two hours to turn everything around before the evening check-in begins at six. Three o'clock is therefore one of the lulls in an otherwise busy day.

'Is everything all right, Madame?' I'd asked.

'Of course, *chérie*,' she'd replied in her strong French accent. 'I have a little surprise for you, that is all.'

At that point, the kitchen door had opened and Jock, the hotel chef, had appeared. In his hand was a plate containing a cupcake with a single lit candle sticking out of it. They'd both serenaded me with a tuneless version of 'Happy Birthday', I'd blown out the candle and Madame had handed me an envelope that I suspected would contain a hundred pounds in cash, because that's what she gave me last year.

I never got the chance to thank her because that was the moment the police stormed the hotel. It was extraordinary; one minute, the three of us were quietly celebrating my birthday, and the next, there were people in black uniforms everywhere, shouting at us not to move.

They've charged Madame with keeping a brothel and controlling prostitution for gain, and Jock and I have been charged as accessories. I was so shocked that I hardly noticed the handcuffs going on, and I meekly let an officer lead me out into the lobby.

One night, not long after I'd started at Hotel Dufour, the fire alarm had developed a fault and went off just after two in the morning. The scene in the lobby as the police officer had led me through reminded me of that event. It was a chaotic tableau of angry, partly dressed guests who had obviously been woken from their sleep, along with several members of the housekeeping team. Exchange the police uniforms for the fire brigade and it could have been a repeat. As we drove away, I could see several of the guests and housekeepers being bundled into vans.

For some reason, all I could think about was Madame. Although she's a forceful personality who can reduce a member of staff to jelly with a single rebuke, she's physically frail, and the shock of her hotel being raided and us being arrested could be enough to trigger a heart attack or stroke.

Now that it's made itself known, my bladder is upping the ante to the point that I can't think about anything else. I try jiggling my legs to relieve the pressure, but something is going to have to give. I stare at the toilet; it's a stainless-steel, all-in-one affair with an integral wash basin, and it's securely bolted down, presumably in case I decide to try and smash up the cell with it. It's no good; burly man or no burly man, I need to go. I hurry over to it, yank down my skirt and knickers and wince at the sensation of the cold steel on my bum as I sit down. Carefully arranging my blouse to preserve my modesty as best I can, I breathe a sigh of relief as I let go.

No sooner have I wiped myself, pulled up my knickers and skirt and washed my hands than the shutter in the door snaps open. 'They're ready to interview you, Beatrice,' a female police officer tells me. 'Please stay away from the door while I open it.'

'Were you watching me?' I ask suspiciously. The timing is just too convenient for it to be a coincidence.

'Did we know you were using the lavatory? Yes, but we can't see anything untoward, don't worry. The camera pixelates the area round the lavatory to protect your privacy.'

I'm not sure that makes me feel any better, but I stand obediently against the bed as the door opens and the policewoman enters the cell, along with the custody officer who booked me in. She's not one of the officers who arrested me or took my details when I arrived here, but I have no idea how many people would work in a place like this. I hold out my hands like I've seen people doing on TV to make it easier for her to put the handcuffs on.

'I'm not going to cuff you, Beatrice.' She smiles. 'You're not planning on giving me any trouble, are you?'

'No. Absolutely not,' I assure her.

'Good.'

The custody officer glances at the clipboard in his hand. 'Can I just confirm that you have declined to have a solicitor present during your interview?'

'That's correct,' I tell him. I'm still riddled with doubt about whether I've done the right thing in turning down a solicitor. On the one hand, it seems foolish to be going into the lion's den without someone there to have my back, but I also wonder whether asking for a solicitor makes you seem more guilty. On the TV dramas, suspects only demand a solicitor when the police start to bring up clear evidence of their crime. Then, when the solicitor arrives, the suspect immediately starts answering all the remaining questions with 'no comment', which only confirms their guilt. I know I haven't done anything wrong, so in the end, I decided to dispense with the solicitor.

'You're in interview room three,' the custody officer informs me as if I'm supposed to know where that is.

'Turn right out of the door,' the policewoman instructs. 'We'll be right behind you.'

As we make our way down the brightly lit corridor, Gary obviously hears us because a fearsome commotion starts up behind one of the other cell doors. He's banging on it with all his might and shouting, 'Let me out, you bastards!'

'Calm down, Gary,' the police officer calls. 'We're very busy right now, so you'll have to wait your turn.'

Gary obviously doesn't like that answer, as the intensity of the banging only increases.

'Left at the end, through the door and then up the stairs,' the policewoman's voice says behind me. I follow her instructions and find myself in front of another door.

'Stand to one side, please,' she instructs before swiping a card through a slot next to the door. I'm expecting a loud buzz as it unlocks, but there's just a soft click and then she holds it open for me to step through. I find myself in another corridor, but this one has a thin carpet and the doors on each side are wooden office-type ones rather than the steel of the cells.

'Third on the right is you,' the policewoman tells me, repeating the procedure with her card when we reach the door. The room I'm shown into is exactly the same as the ones I've seen on TV. There's a small table with two chairs on each side, and a screen fixed to the wall over the table.

'Take a seat on the far side,' the policewoman instructs. 'They won't be long. Would you like a cup of tea or anything?'

'A cup of tea would be lovely, thank you,' I reply, making sure to sound as grateful and obsequious as possible. This is obviously a mix-up of some description, but I'm wise enough to realise that stomping around arrogantly asserting my rights is just going to get their backs up.

The door closes with a soft click and I can hear the lock engage. I'm alone again. The weird thing is that I'm not scared. The arrest itself was such a whirlwind, I didn't really have time to feel anything, but I'm so certain they'll realise this is all a massive mistake that it hasn't occurred to me to be frightened. I know some London hotels turn a blind eye to prostitution; I've heard all the stories about guests phoning down for a coded 'extra pillow', or concierges who are in cahoots with various escort agencies, but I'm certain that Madame would never permit anything so sordid. Plus, I'm pretty sure I'd have spotted it if anything like that was going on. I spend quite a lot of time around the reception area, so I'd notice random young women having meetings with their 'uncles', which is another giveaway.

I have no idea what time it is, I realise. I could have been here for thirty minutes, but it could equally be three hours. I haven't seen daylight since I arrived as there was no window in my cell, and there isn't one in here either. They also relieved me of my phone when they booked me in, so I have no way of telling the time. I wonder if taking away all the normal indicators that tell us where we are in the day is a subtle ruse to confuse prisoners and make them more likely to confess.

I'm still pondering this when the lock clicks, the door opens, and two plain clothes police officers enter the room, one male and one female.

'Sorry to keep you, Beatrice,' the female officer says, pushing a plastic disposable cup across the table towards me as she and her colleague take their seats. 'I'm Detective Inspector Winter, and this is my colleague, Detective Sergeant Hollis. Are you ready to begin?'

'I am,' I tell her.

'Great. I'll just start the recording and then we can get down to business,' she informs me as she reaches out and presses a menu item on the screen.

'No tape recorder?' I ask.

'Goodness no. We're digital now. Welcome to the twenty-first century.' She smiles and then taps an icon.

'Interview with Beatrice Fairhead,' she says in a monotone. 'Seventeenth of April 2023, time is six fifteen p.m. In the room are Miss Fairhead, DI Winter and DS Hollis.'

'Beatrice, you are being interviewed under caution,' DS Hollis informs me. 'I'm going to repeat what that means for the recording. You have been arrested on suspicion of being an accessory to keeping a brothel and controlling prostitution for gain. You do not have to say anything, but it may harm your defence if you do not mention when questioned something which you later rely on in court. Anything you do say may be given in evidence. Do you understand?'

'Yes,' I tell him.

'And can you confirm for the recording that you have declined to have a solicitor present during this interview?' he continues.

'I can.'

'Great stuff,' DI Winter says, as if I've just won the star prize at school. 'Let's start at the beginning. How long have you known Eileen Strickland?'

Who?

2

———

'I'm sorry,' I tell them as carefully as I can. 'I think there must be some mistake. I don't know anyone called Eileen Strickland.'

'Let's not play games,' DS Hollis says abruptly. 'She was literally standing next to you at the moment of your arrest.'

'That was Madame Dufour,' I insist.

DI Winter laughs softly. 'Of course. I keep forgetting that's what she's calling herself now. Fine. Tell us about your relationship with Madame Dufour.'

'She's the owner of the hotel where I work. I'm her hotel manager.'

'I see. And how long have you worked there?'

'Just under two years.'

'So you would have been twenty-six when you started?'

'Twenty-seven. It's my birthday today.'

'Of course it is. Many happy returns. Forgive my ignorance, but is it normal for hotel managers to be so young?'

'No, but I have more experience than most people my age. My parents own a small hotel in Ludlow, so I've grown up in the business. My degree is in hospitality and I've been working in the industry from the moment I graduated.'

'Where were you working before Hotel Dufour?'

'I was assistant manager at The Old Stable Yard in Islington.'

'Hm. I don't know that one.'

'It's not there any more. It went under.'

'Check it out, will you, DS Hollis?' DI Winter instructs, and he writes it on his pad.

'OK, so how did you get the position at Hotel Dufour? Did you approach Eileen, I mean Madame Dufour, or did she approach you?'

'When I found out that The Old Stable Yard was closing, I signed on with an agency that specialises in the hospitality industry. They sent my CV to Madame Dufour, among others. She interviewed me and contacted me a couple of days later to offer me the position. It was a step up from my previous job, the pay was good and onsite accommodation was included, so it was a no-brainer.'

'And you didn't have any suspicions about her? Nothing about her seemed off in any way?'

'No. I mean, she's a little old-fashioned, I suppose, but she runs a tight ship.'

'Old-fashioned? Can you give an example?'

'She insists that the beds are made up with sheets and blankets. I suggested to her once, early on before I knew what she was like, that most people slept under duvets these days and they might prefer them. Plus it would make life easier for the housekeeping staff.'

'That sounds reasonable. What did she say?'

'She was furious. She told me there was no way her guests were going to sleep on glorified dog beds, like animals, and she wasn't in business to make life easier for the housekeepers.'

'Never a truer word spoken,' DS Hollis mutters under his breath.

'Let's turn our attention to the housekeepers for a moment,' DI Winter continues. 'How many rooms do you have in the hotel?'

'Forty-eight.'

'And, if I understand correctly, there are twelve housekeepers. That seems a lot to me. Is it?'

'It is a lot, but we usually have to turn the rooms over twice a day, so it's a greater workload than most hotels.'

'I assume part of your role is supervising the housekeeping staff?'

'No. They're under Maria, the head of housekeeping. I spot check a bedroom every so often, but Maria is very protective of her domain, so I have to be careful not to tread on her toes too much.'

'Is that usual?'

'No, but Madame and Maria go way back, apparently, and Madame trusts her implicitly.'

'So, just to clarify,' DI Winter continues in her conversational tone. 'Maria is in charge of the housekeeping staff and, beyond the odd bedroom inspection, you have nothing to do with them?'

'That's correct.'

'Tell me about your clientele,' she says. 'Are they mostly repeat customers, or are they mainly one-offs?'

'A lot of them are regulars.'

'And when you say regular, how regular? Once a week? Once a month?'

'It varies. Some guests are members of our subscription plan, and they might stay several times a week. Others less frequent. They also divide between those who stay with us overnight and those who use the siesta service.'

'OK, there's a lot of information in there that I'd like to unpack, if you don't mind. What is the subscription plan?'

'The best way of describing it is like being a member of a gym. You pay a subscription, and that entitles you to a number of stays each month. It works out cheaper than if you were just to book the room and, if you subscribe to the overnight package, you get dinner and breakfast included.'

'And, like the gym, a good workout is guaranteed,' DS Hollis observes wryly.

'Thank you, DS Hollis,' DI Winter says firmly before turning back to me. 'And what is the siesta service?'

'That's our afternoon package, for people who just need to catch a few hours of sleep in the middle of the day. A lot of our guests have demanding jobs where they need to be in the office at antisocial hours, so an afternoon kip keeps their energy levels up.'

'And are these things normal for a hotel to offer?' DS Hollis asks.

'Many hotels have loyalty schemes and, although the siesta service is unusual, we're not unique in offering it. It's a way to maximise the revenue from each room and the entire hospitality industry is looking for innovative ways to make the most of their assets these days. Margins are tight, so every little helps.'

'I think there's a considerable difference between, say, a Hilton Honours card and the kind of loyalty scheme you were offering,' DS Hollis challenges. I can see he's playing the bad cop to DI Winter's good cop, and I decide I don't like him at all.

'I don't think that's a fair comparison,' I reply, trying to keep my voice light. 'Our offering would be better compared to being a member of one of the London clubs.'

This is obviously too much for DS Hollis. 'Are you seriously trying to compare your squalid little brothel to the RAC club, or the Garrick?'

'Why are you so convinced that Hotel Dufour is a brothel?' I ask.

'We'll come to that,' DI Winter says, shooting her colleague a warning look. 'Tell me a little bit more about your guests. Is there an equal split of men and women, or does one gender feature more prominently?'

'It's almost exclusively men,' I tell her.

'Doesn't that strike you as odd?'

'Not really. Madame Dufour has been targeting a specific demographic.'

'Which is?'

'We're in the heart of the City. We have investment banks, stockbrokers, law firms and the like on our doorstep. They're our target market.'

'And don't women work in any of those industries?'

'They do, but they're still dominated by men.'

'So it doesn't seem unusual to you that your clientele is exclusively male.'

'It isn't *exclusively* male. I just said it was mainly men.'

'You said, and I quote, "It's almost exclusively men",' DS Hollis challenges.

'That's right, but I think that probably reflects the demographic of our target market.'

'Fine.' DI Winters takes over again. 'Let's move on to your domestic arrangements. You said accommodation was included?'

'That's right. The top floor is set aside for staff, and I have a room there.'

'Is that usual?'

'It's not unusual.'

'Who else lives onsite?'

'Madame, obviously. Maria and Jock.'

'Jock?'

'The hotel chef.'

She consults her notes. 'You mean Andrew McLaughlin.'

'Yes, but everyone calls him Jock because he's Scottish. It's a nickname, like calling him Paddy if he was Irish.'

'It seems like everybody in this place is hiding under a false name.' DS Hollis sighs. 'Why would a chef need to live onsite?'

'Because Madame likes him to be available at all times, in case a guest wants a sandwich or something in the middle of the night.'

'Does that happen a lot? Your clientele waking at two in the morning with the munchies?' he asks, and I spot him writing the word 'drugs' in large letters on his pad, with a question mark afterwards.

'Not to my knowledge,' I tell him firmly, anxious to shut down that line of enquiry. If Madame finds out the police think she's been dealing drugs on top of whatever misinformation they're already working with, it could give her a coronary.

'Why offer it then?'

'Because it's what all the good hotels do. If you have guests that have come from abroad, for example, they may be jetlagged and want to eat at strange times of the day.'

'But you've just told me that international guests aren't your target market.' DS Hollis is obviously determined not to let this go.

'They aren't, but that doesn't mean we shouldn't cater for them. It's also something we charge a premium for, because it's out-of-hours service, same as shoe shine and overnight laundry.'

'What kind of premium?' DI Winter asks. 'If I wanted a bacon sandwich at two in the morning, what would I be looking at?'

'Twenty-five pounds, plus twelve and a half per cent service charge.'

'Bloody hell, I'm in the wrong job.'

'It's not unusual for hotels to upsell to their guests,' I tell her.

'Certainly not in your case,' DS Hollis retorts.

I've had enough of his smart remarks. 'Are you going to tell me what this is about?' I ask him, trying and failing not to sound tetchy.

DS Hollis looks at DI Winter, who gives him an almost imperceptible nod.

'With pleasure,' he says. 'Your precious Madame Dufour is, as we previously mentioned, better known as Eileen Strickland, to the police at least. She has a string of criminal convictions as long as my arm, dating back to the 1960s, and has done several stints in prison.'

'No,' I tell him. 'You must have her mixed up with someone else. Madame would never—'

'There's no mix up, I can assure you.' He taps the screen a few times and a grainy mugshot of a young woman appears. Although it must have been taken many years ago, it's clearly Madame. I'm gobsmacked and just stare at it in silence.

'This is from her first arrest, for prostitution,' he continues after I've studied the picture for a little while. 'She was arrested a number of times between 1968 and 1974 for the same offence, but obviously started to lose her allure as time went by and had to seek out new income streams.' He swipes the screen and another picture of Madame appears, looking slightly older.

'This is the first time she received a custodial sentence, in 1975,' DS Hollis informs me. 'Funnily enough, it was for running a brothel. After her release, she turned her hand to pornography, and was arrested again in 1981 under the Obscene Publications Act.' He swipes the screen to reveal yet another picture.

'Just because someone has a shady past doesn't mean everything they do is against the law,' I protest.

'Indeed not, but you can understand why we might have been interested. We placed an undercover officer in the hotel, posing as a guest. What do you think happened?'

'I would hope he or she had an enjoyable stay and gave us a positive review on TripAdvisor.'

'Lose the attitude. You're not funny,' DS Hollis snarls. 'You know as well as I do that no sooner had he called to ask for an extra pillow than a member of your so-called housekeeping team knocked on his door to offer him a smorgasbord of sexual services. Are you seriously trying to tell me that all this was going on under your nose and you didn't have a clue?'

'Of course I didn't!' I exclaim, my heart now thudding uncomfortably in my chest.

'Why did you have all that cash on you when we arrested you?'

'It was my birthday present from Madame!' I'm aware that I'm raising my voice to match his, and I remind myself to keep calm and not wind them up.

'Here's the problem, Beatrice. I don't believe a word you're saying,' DS Hollis counters. 'In your own words, you've just told us that there are a number of aspects of this so-called "hotel" that should have raised red flags, but you expect us to believe you didn't suspect anything untoward was going on? You're either fantastically naïve or an accomplished liar. Which is it?'

I'm aware of the tears starting to fall down my cheeks as I look at them imploringly. 'I didn't know a thing, I promise,' I tell them.

'Interview terminated,' he sighs eventually. 'Time is six forty-five. Wait here, Beatrice, until the custody officer comes to take you back to your cell.' They both stand, and the door clicks softly behind them, leaving me alone in the room again.

For the first time, it dawns on me quite how much trouble I'm in. Stupid, arrogant Beatrice, thinking the police had made a mistake. I should have asked for a solicitor. I might be telling the truth, but that means nothing if they don't believe it. I stare at the cold, untouched cup of tea as the tears pour down my cheeks and drip off my chin.

3

I've cried myself out and I must have dozed off, because the clang of the shutter opening starts me awake.

'Stay well back from the door,' the same police officer from earlier tells me. We repeat the journey to the interview room and, after a short wait, DS Hollis and DI Winter come in and sit opposite me again.

'OK,' DI Winter says. 'Here is what we're going to do. DS Hollis and I agree that, although there are a number of holes in your story, it's not enough to charge you at this point. So we're going to release you on bail, pending further investigation. What that means is that you will be taken back to your residence by a police officer, and you will surrender your passport to that officer. You must be at your residence between the hours of 7 p.m. and 7 a.m. Do you understand?'

I'm so relieved that it's all I can do not to stand and punch the air. 'Yes,' I say meekly.

'You will report back here at 10 a.m. next Monday, the twenty-fourth. At that time, we will tell you whether we are going to charge you or not. If you do not keep the conditions of your bail, or you fail to report at the time set, we will issue a warrant for your arrest. Do you understand?'

'Yes.'

'Good. I'll take you to the front desk, where the custody officer will book you out and we'll return all your possessions apart from your phone. We need to keep that as evidence for the time being. Do you have any questions before we go?'

'No.' I'm anxious to get out of here as quickly as possible, before they change their minds. DI Winter leads me back to the desk where I was booked in and, after I've signed the forms, my keys and the envelope with my birthday money from Madame is returned.

'Take a seat over there,' the custody officer instructs, pointing to a row of chairs by the door. 'I'll let you know when the car is here to take you back.'

I do as I'm told and, a few moments later, the door to the custody suite opens and Jock appears. After going through the same process, he sits down next to me.

'Are you OK?' he murmurs.

'I've been better. You?'

He sighs. 'It's been pretty intense.'

'Your carriage awaits,' the custody officer informs us cheerfully, pointing through the glass doorway to an unmarked police car, although the driver's uniform gives the game away somewhat. 'We'll see you next week. Don't be late.' He smiles, but I'm not in the mood for humour.

Neither Jock nor I utter a word to each other on the journey back; both of us are lost in our thoughts.

'I'm going to drop you at the rear entrance,' the police officer explains as we approach the hotel. 'Word has got out, as it always does, and there are a number of individuals from the press staking out the front. I suggest you keep a low profile.'

He's not wrong. As we drive past the hotel, I can see a couple of police officers guarding the front door, and there's a TV van and a number of people wielding long-lensed cameras on the other side of the road. Unfortunately, they've outmanoeuvred us, and there are a few outside the back door as well. No sooner has the car pulled up than cameras are being shoved in our faces and I'm temporarily blinded as the flashes go off. They're shouting questions but I concentrate on keeping my head down as the police officer bundles us towards the rear entrance. My hands are shaking and it takes me a few goes to get the key in the lock, but then we're in the kitchen. Such was the speed of our departure that nobody has turned the light off, and we stand there, blinking for a moment or two as our eyes adjust to the brightness.

'OK,' the police officer says. 'I'm going to ask you to accompany me to the lobby and lock the front doors. That will allow our officers to stand down. I will then wait here while you fetch your passports, and I'll leave you in peace once you've surrendered them.'

I normally make a rule of climbing the stairs to my room, telling myself that the exercise is good for me, but I don't have the energy today, so I insert my key in the slot in the lift that unlocks the top floor, and Jock and I ride up in silence. As soon as I step into my room, I can tell something isn't right. It looks broadly the same as when I left it this morning, but a few objects are in the wrong places. The police must have searched it, I realise. Thankfully, it only takes me a moment to locate my passport, but I have to wait a few minutes before Jock reappears and we take the lift back down.

'Sorry,' he says. 'It wasn't where I thought it was.'

'Did they search your room too?'

'It looks like it.'

After handing us a receipt, the police officer warns us again about the curfew, as well as not entering any of the guest bedrooms in case they need to get forensic evidence from them, and then he's gone and it's just the two of us.

'I don't know about you,' Jock says with a weak smile, 'but I could really use a drink. Would you care to join me in the bar?'

'I don't think Madame would like that,' I say automatically.

'Eileen, you mean? Oddly, after what I've been through today, I struggle to give a shit what she thinks. I'm going to have a large Scotch. Are you coming?'

I dither for a moment. It feels wrong and unprofessional but, on reflection, I realise that Jock has a point and I could do with something stronger than tea after the ordeal I've just been through.

'You're right,' I tell him. 'Lead the way.'

The bar is in darkness apart from the glow coming from the till, and I'm careful to pull the heavy damask curtains across the windows before turning on the lights. The last thing we need is to be spotted by any passing paparazzi.

'Did you suspect?' he asks as I follow him over to one of the tables in the bar, having poured him a generous measure of whisky and filled a glass almost to the brim with red wine for me.

'Not a thing. You?'

'Nope. I just thought she was a pernickety old woman with an eighties food obsession. I mean, who even eats duck *à l'orange* any more? We must be the only place in London still serving this stuff.'

'Technically, she'd call it *canard à l'orange*. French is more *sophistiqué*.'

'Yeah, like *petits pois à la Parisienne*, otherwise known as ponced-up peas and carrots.' He laughs.

'And a generous helping of *croquettes de pommes de terre*.' I'm laughing too. I'm sure it's just the release of tension, but it feels good.

'Otherwise known as deep-fried mashed potato,' Jock howls.

'Don't forget the silver service. In on the left, out on the right, don't stack the plates,' I add, barely able to breathe for laughing.

'It just doesn't add up, does it?' Jock says when we've laughed out the stress and recovered our composure. 'Such a stickler for detail down here, while all along up there...' He pauses, lost in thought. 'Do you think the girls were coerced?'

'I can't think of any woman who would go into sex work if she had alternatives,' I tell him. 'I'm still struggling to come to terms with it though. Alicja, for example. She's so delicate that she bursts into tears if Maria so much as looks at her crossly. I can't marry that up with the other things Madame must have expected her to do.'

He ponders for a moment. 'I hate her,' he says.

'Yeah. If this is true, and what the police showed me this afternoon would indicate that it is, I hate her too.'

We sip our drinks in silence, contemplating the enormity of Madame's deceit. After a while, I get up and bring both the scotch and wine bottles over to the table so I can refill our glasses. Jock stares at me thoughtfully.

'What?' I ask him when his gaze starts to make me uncomfortable.

'Sorry. I was just trying to work you out,' Jock says after taking a large mouthful of whisky.

'What do you mean?'

'Don't take this the wrong way, but I've always seen you as Madame's little enforcer, continually on the lookout for an excuse to pick up people's mistakes.'

'There's nothing wrong with being good at my job and having high standards,' I tell him fiercely. Unfortunately, the wine has started to go to my head so it comes out slightly slurred. I make a note to slow down a little. Today's been bad enough without me getting drunk and vomiting my guts all over the place.

'Sorry. I wasn't trying to upset you. It's just that we've never really chatted before, and I'm seeing a different side of you tonight. I'll admit that I've always thought you were a bit uptight, but you're OK, you know that?'

'Why thank you, I think.' I smile and chink our glasses before taking another sip.

'What are you going to do?' I ask him after another pause. 'I think we can assume this place won't be reopening any time soon.'

'I might go back to Scotland,' he replies after thinking about it for a while. 'I like London, but I think I need some time back home after this. You?'

'I'll get in touch with the agency again. Hopefully, something will come up soon. That's assuming the police don't convince themselves I'm in cahoots with Madame, in which case it won't matter because I'll be behind bars.'

'I reckon they know we're innocent. There's a reason why we're here and Madame and Maria aren't, don't you think?'

'Do you think Maria was in on it too?'

'She must have been. She was directly in charge of the house-keeping team, wasn't she.'

'Bloody hell,' I murmur.

Our thoughts are interrupted by the distant sound of a telephone.

'It's the main switchboard,' I say to Jock as I get to my feet. 'I'd better get it.'

'Leave it,' he suggests. 'We're closed.'

'What if it's the police, wanting to check we haven't absconded?'

'Fine. Answer it then.'

I hurry out into the reception area, which is also in near darkness. It's eerie out here, and I wish I'd asked Jock to come with me.

'It's quite safe. Nobody's going to jump out at you,' I tell myself before lifting the receiver and carefully saying, 'Hotel Dufour, how may I help?'

'Oh yeah, hi,' the male voice on the other end says. 'My name is Robin Bugg, from the *Morning Post*. I was wondering if you would mind answering a few questions. Can I take your name, for the record?'

'No, and I have nothing to say to the press,' I tell him, putting on my most officious tone. 'Goodbye.'

No sooner have I hung up than the phone rings again. The stress of the afternoon combines with the wine I've drunk to tip me over the edge, and I snatch up the receiver angrily.

'I said *I'm not talking to the press*,' I snarl belligerently. 'Piss off and leave us alone.'

'Beatrice, is that you?' I'd recognise that voice anywhere. Even after thirty years of living in the UK, my mother still has a vestige of a Spanish accent. My relationship with my parents is best described as distant, so I'm momentarily dumbfounded that she's rung at all, especially using the main switchboard.

'Oh, hello, Mum. Sorry about that, I thought you were a journalist,' I say quickly. Mum doesn't approve of what she calls 'coarse language'.

'What's going on, Beatrice?' she asks anxiously. 'We've just seen you on the news. Did you know what that woman was doing?'

'Of course I didn't know!' I exclaim. 'Wait, what do you mean I was on the news?'

'It was the leading item on the ten o'clock news. Police raided and shut down a brothel that was hiding in plain sight, pretending to be a hotel. They showed pictures of you and a young man being escorted by a policeman. I tried your mobile but it just kept going to voicemail. We were worried.'

The accusing tone of her last sentence washes over me as I digest the information. The pictures by the back door. I should have known they'd be sold on instantly.

'Sorry,' I tell her. 'The police have confiscated my phone.'

'Why? Have you been *arrested*?' She sounds absolutely horrified.

'All the staff were interviewed under caution,' I explain quickly. I don't know if it's true, but I know she'll feel better if she thinks it was just a routine thing. 'But they let me go, so it's fine.' I decide not to tell her that I'm officially on bail; there's no way she'll be able to cope with that.

'You poor darling, do you need to come home? Oh, hang on a minute, your father is saying something. What is it, Rod?'

I listen to my parents' muffled voices while I try to think up a plausible story about why I can't go home right now, without mentioning that I'm under curfew and might still go to prison.

'Sorry about that, darling,' Mum says as she comes back on the line. 'Your father feels, well, we both feel that it might be best if you didn't come home *right now*, on reflection. You're something of a *celebrity* at the moment, and please don't take this the wrong way because we love you *desperately*, but you might draw the wrong kind of attention to us. I'm sure it will all blow over in a few weeks and then we'd love to see you, of course. You understand, don't you?'

Bloody hell, that's a low blow, even from them.

'Of course I understand,' I tell her flatly. I don't know why I'm upset; it's not as if I could have gone anyway, even if I'd wanted to, which I don't.

'I knew you would,' she gushes. 'OK, well if there's anything we can do, just let us know. I expect you're exhausted after all your adventures, so I'll let you get to bed. Bye darling, love you.'

'Bye, Mum,' I say, but she's already hung up. As soon as I put the phone down, it starts ringing again, so I take it off the hook and walk back into the bar.

'Who was it?' Jock asks as I take a large mouthful of wine.

'My mother. Apparently, we were the lead item on the news, along with the pictures those bastards took of us coming in the back door. She's asked me not to go home in case I taint them by association.'

'What?' He sounds appalled.

'Don't worry. It's not a surprise. It's kind of par for the course from my parents.'

'I'm sorry.'

'Thanks.'

Jock has been here longer than me but, as we sip our drinks in silence, I realise I've never looked at him properly before. I mean, I've looked at him, obviously, but I haven't really noticed him. Physically, we couldn't be more different, and it's not just because he's a man and much taller than me. Where I've definitely inherited my dark hair, brown eyes and olive complexion from my mother, Jock is fair haired with bright-blue eyes that sit above a perfectly straight nose. When he smiles, his teeth are even and white. He's actually quite good looking, now that I'm seeing him as a person rather than just the head chef. He's obviously noticed me gazing at him because his face turns quizzical all of a sudden and I feel my cheeks heating up in embarrassment that he caught me staring so brazenly.

'It's late,' I tell him to defuse the sudden tension in the air. 'We probably ought to go to bed.'

'You're right,' he says, picking up the bottles and putting them back on the bar.

We ride the lift up in silence, and then wish each other good-night before disappearing into our rooms. As I brush my teeth in my tiny ensuite shower room, I contemplate my conversation with Jock. That was probably the most we've spoken since I've been here, but he seems like a nice guy. There are many worse people I could have been incarcerated with for a week, I think as a big yawn catches me by surprise. At least I should sleep well tonight; I'm absolutely exhausted.

4

I may be absolutely exhausted, but sleep is firmly refusing to come. I've tried thinking happy thoughts, but they're quickly overwhelmed by images of people in my bedroom going through all my personal stuff. I feel spied on and violated. I remember some burglary victims talking on TV ages ago about how it was the idea of the burglars in their house going through their things that was almost more upsetting than the loss of the stolen items. It seemed odd to me back then, but I fully understand what they mean now. Every time I close my eyes, visions of policemen going through my drawers start playing in my mind and I have to open them again to banish the images.

I've also never been this alone in the hotel before. There has always been life around me – guests sleeping (or not, as I've learned today) and the reassurance that the night porter is keeping an eye on everything – but now there's nothing. However, even though Jock and I are the only ones here, it isn't quiet. The faint hum of traffic below is familiar, but now my heart quickens every time I hear a siren, which happens a lot in London. There are also occasional creaks and bangs within the building, and my imagination starts conjuring up wild interpretations of what they might be. At one point, I manage to convince myself there's someone tiptoeing along the corridor outside my room and I pull the duvet over my head for protection like I used to do when I was a child. As carefully as I can, I reach for my bedside light, snapping it on with one hand while wrenching the duvet off my head with the other, in the hope of startling whoever I've now decided is in my room for long enough to make my escape. Of course, there's nobody there. My fight or flight impulse has kicked in fully though, and I sit on the edge of the bed waiting for my heart and breathing to slow down.

I glance at my bedside clock; it's just after half past one in the morning and there's no way I'm going to be able to sleep at this rate. I'd almost feel safer in the cell at the custody suite, which I know is ridiculous. I decide to make myself a cup of herbal tea. Although our rooms all have ensuite bathrooms, like the guest rooms on the floors below, we also have a communal sitting room and kitchen up here. My heart is thudding again as I carefully open my bedroom door. The corridor lighting is dimmed to save energy, but it's enough for me to reassure myself there's nobody else out here. To my left is the door to Madame's suite of rooms. I've never been in there, but Maria told me once that her suite is made up of four guest rooms, knocked about to give her a palatial bedroom and bathroom, with a large sitting room to boot. Apparently, the decoration is so lavish, it wouldn't look out of place at the Palais de Versailles.

I'm briefly tempted to have a nose, but I quickly realise that would be a suicidal thing to do. If the police come back and find evidence that I've been in Madame's room, that's going to make me look guilty as hell. I've seen enough of those true crime documentaries to know that even a single hair would be enough for the forensic team to place me in there. With a shudder, I turn right towards the kitchen. After flipping on the light and filling the kettle, I select a chamomile tea in the hope it will help me relax and get to sleep. The sound of the kettle heating is deafening in the silence, and I've just added the boiling water to my mug when Jock appears in a T-shirt and boxer shorts, looking dishevelled.

'Are you OK?' he asks.

'Sorry, I didn't mean to wake you.'

'Don't worry, I was awake anyway.'

'Do you want a chamomile tea?'

'No, you're all right. I'm more of a builder's tea man, and I don't think one of those would do me any good at this time of night. I'll just grab myself a glass of water.'

I settle myself at the table and watch as he gets a glass out of the cupboard and fills it from the tap, before coming and sitting opposite me. Neither of us speaks for a while, but the silence has a comfortable quality to it, like it does when you know someone so well, you don't need to speak to be understood. In a way, I'm not surprised. We've both been through the same horrible experience, we're both facing an uncertain future and we've both been spectacularly deceived.

'I don't think I've ever seen you with your hair down before,' he observes after a while. 'It suits you.'

I run my hand through my hair self-consciously. I always wear it up in a bun with a hair doughnut when I'm working; it's part of my professional persona. I'm starting to feel mildly uncomfortable under Jock's gaze; I'm not used to people seeing me out of my work 'uniform' of dark pencil skirt with matching jacket and white blouse, so I feel a bit vulnerable in my long sleep shirt with only a pair of knickers underneath. I know I'm perfectly decent, but it feels intimate, somehow, especially as he's not wearing much either.

'So, what was keeping you awake?' Jock asks, diverting me from my mounting unease.

'Every time I close my eyes, my mind seems to go into over-drive. I'm exhausted but also totally wired.'

'I know exactly what you mean.'

'I never realised this building was so noisy either. Did it sound to you like there was someone walking along the corridor earlier?'

'I can't say that I noticed, sorry. I was busy imagining myself in prison.'

'You're a big guy, I'm sure you'd be able to take care of your-self,' I tell him with a small smile.

He grins. 'I guess there's a compliment lurking in there.' As he drains his glass and stands up, my eyes are instantly drawn to his thighs, which are as thick as tree trunks and dusted with light-brown hair. Men with totally hairless legs look unnatural, in my view, but the gorilla look doesn't do it for me either. Jock's legs are just right. Why the hell am I thinking about his legs? *Get a grip, Beatrice.*

'Right, I'm going to try again,' he tells me. 'See you in the morning.'

As soon as he's gone, I feel my anxiety levels start to rise again. I take the chamomile tea back to my bedroom, but I'm no more relaxed by the time I've finished it. The clock tells me it's now two in the morning. What am I going to do? I remember how I used to climb into Mum and Dad's bed if I got really scared in the night as a child. They always complained, but I'd burrow in between them anyway and feel perfectly safe.

The thought comes to me totally unbidden and I dismiss it straight away. The problem with thoughts like this one is that they're not so easily fobbed off. I can't do it; Jock would think I was either coming on to him or a lunatic. The idea is ignoring my objections though, and pretty soon I can't think of anything else. With a growl, I grab my pillow and walk out into the hallway, knocking gently on Jock's door.

After a second or so, he opens it a crack and peers out at me.

'What's up?' he asks.

'This is going to sound crazy,' I tell him. 'In fact, it is crazy. Forget I came.' I turn to go back to my room.

'Why are you holding your pillow?'

I sigh. 'It's stupid. I was just thinking about how I used to sleep in Mum and Dad's bedroom if I got scared in the night when I was little.'

'And you're scared tonight.'

I nod.

'You'd better come in then,' he says, holding the door open.

'This isn't a sex thing. You know that, right?'

'It's fine, Beatrice. Are you coming or not?'

'Are you sure you don't mind?'

'I wouldn't be holding the door open if I did.'

I step into his room. Normally, I'd be consumed with curiosity and want to take in every detail, but it's hard to see much in the dim glow of his bedside light.

'I normally sleep on the left,' he tells me.

'That's handy,' I say self-consciously. 'I sleep on the right.'

'Jump in then.'

I slip under the duvet and lie down on my back, averting my gaze as he clambers in next to me and turns off the light. This feels very strange and uncomfortable and I'm just contemplating getting up and going back to my room when his hand finds mine in the darkness and gives it a squeeze.

'You're safe now,' he whispers. 'Close your eyes and go to sleep.'

I roll over onto my side and I'm fast asleep within seconds.

* * *

OK, this is super awkward. I slept like a baby with Jock beside me but, when I wake the next morning, we appear to be spooned together and Jock's arm is around my midriff. His breathing is deep and even, which tells me he's still asleep, so I start to plan how I can escape from his grip without waking him up. Very slowly, I start to ease my way out from under his arm, but he obviously senses the movement because he pulls me back in.

To be fair, there are worse places to be. I haven't shared a bed with anyone since I was at university so it's a long time since anyone has held me like this. I'd forgotten how nice it feels. Maybe I'll just stay here for a little while longer. After all, it's not like there's anything urgent I need to be doing. There's no breakfast service to supervise, no guests to check out. I can't even start job hunting until I know whether I'm going to prison or not.

The thought of prison sends a shudder down my spine, and I have to give myself a shake to get rid of it. Jock yawns behind me and stretches his legs. There's no bedside clock on my side of the bed, so I have no idea what time it is.

'Oh shit, I am so sorry,' Jock's says as he hastily removes his arm and shuffles his body away from mine. I take the opportunity to roll over and look at him. He's puce with embarrassment.

'It's fine,' I reassure him. 'In fact, it was probably what I needed. I can't remember the last time I slept so solidly. Did you sleep OK? I hope I didn't fidget too much.'

'I went out like a light. I really am sorry though. I don't know what came over me.'

'Don't blame yourself. After all, we don't know who spooned who. It might have been me, and you just put your arm round me as a reflex. The point is that I felt safe, so thank you for taking me in. I know it was a bizarre request.'

This seems to cheer him up, and he rolls over to look at his bedside clock.

'Bloody hell, half past seven,' he announces. 'I haven't slept in this late for years.'

'Me neither.'

An uneasy silence falls, and I feel we're both searching for a phrase to lift the awkwardness of being in the same bed when we really don't know each other that well.

'Umm, I suppose I'd better go back to my room and think about getting up properly,' I say eventually, as I swing my legs out of the bed. 'Thank you for having me.'

To my surprise, Jock bursts out laughing.

'What?'

'Thank you for having me,' he parrots. 'It's just so... formal. Are you going to write me a thank you letter as well?'

'Piss off,' I say, but I'm laughing too. 'What should I have said then?'

'Something about how sharing a bed with me was a life-changing experience would have been nice.'

'Is that what all the girls say?'

'Not exactly, but a boy can dream.'

'OK, let me try again,' I tell him as I swing my legs back into the bed and lean over towards him.

'You, Jock, are my knight in shining armour,' I tell him, laying it on as thick as I can. 'I was a damsel in distress, and you gallantly came to my rescue. Alas, I have no fortune, but I hope you will accept this kiss as a token of my undying gratitude.'

I lean in further and plant a kiss on his cheek.

'Is that better?' I ask.

'I prefer it to "thank you for having me", even though you were blatantly taking the piss.'

'Good. Right, I'm going to love you and leave you.'

'Shall we meet in the main kitchen in half an hour? I could make us some breakfast.'

I grin. 'That sounds like an excellent idea.'

As I cross the corridor, I glance again at Madame's door and I realise that, although Jock's and my freedom is hanging in the balance, our situation is considerably more promising than hers and Maria's. The thought gives me a lot of comfort, and I'm smiling as I undress and step into the shower.

5

'Good grief, what are you wearing?' Jock exclaims as I enter the kitchen half an hour later.

'What do you mean?' I ask. As I'm off duty, I've put on a faded pair of jeans and a hoodie. I've also left my hair down.

'Sorry, I guess I never saw you as someone who wore casual clothes. What with that and your hair, you look like a completely different person.'

'Do you want me to change into my uniform and put my hair up? I'd hate to traumatise you.'

'No, it's fine. Sorry, I should have thought before opening my mouth. I meant it as a compliment, but it came out wrong.'

'You don't exactly look like a chef this morning either,' I observe, waving my hand at his jeans and T-shirt combo.

Our fashion debate is interrupted by the sound of the back door buzzer and we both glance automatically at the screen showing the CCTV feed. To our relief, it's Ramon with the laundry delivery and not a pack of journalists.

'I guess nobody's told him we're closed,' Jock says.

'Leave it to me. I'll deal with it,' I tell him as I make my way over to the door.

'Once a hotel manager, always a hotel manager,' he calls after me, and I can hear the laughter in his voice.

'Oh, hello, Miss Fairhead,' Ramon says in his heavily accented voice, looking at me curiously. 'You look different today.'

'I'm off duty, Ramon,' I tell him. 'The hotel is closed.'

'Closed? Why?'

'Haven't you seen the news?'

'What for I watch the news? Always the same old thing.'

'OK, well if you had seen it, you would know that we've been closed down by the police because it appears Madame was running this place as a brothel,' I tell him blandly.

'What is a brothel?'

I sigh. I shouldn't be surprised really; it's hardly the sort of word they would teach you in English class.

'It's a place where men pay money to have sex with women,' I explain.

'Oh,' he says, and his face falls. 'That is a bad business. A very bad business.'

'It is. So the police have taken Madame into custody and closed us down. We're not going to need fresh laundry today, I'm afraid.'

'I understand. I will come back tomorrow.'

'We won't want any laundry tomorrow either, Ramon. We're closed for the foreseeable future.'

'Oh.'

He stands there, obviously unsure what to do.

'Look, if the situation changes, we'll let you know, OK?'

He sighs and turns away, dragging the laundry cart back to

his van. I'm sure I hear him mutter 'a very bad business' once more as I close the door.

Jock is still staring at the CCTV feed when I join him again.

'What?' I ask.

'Did you see anyone else out there while you were talking to Ramon?'

'I don't think so. Why?'

'I was just wondering if the paparazzi had lost interest.'

'I expect so. There are probably new, more exciting scandals to cover, like a celebrity accidentally showing a bit of body fat. What's that phrase about today's news being tomorrow's fish and chip paper?'

'I guess you're right. What would you like for breakfast then? I can rustle up a *Petit Dejeuner à l'Anglais* if you want, or *Oeufs à la Bénédictine* if that's a bit much. I could probably even manage an *omelette au fromage et jambon*. That's a cheese and ham omelette to anyone who isn't Madame.'

Normally, the idea of a full English breakfast would make me feel decidedly queasy; I've never been able to understand how someone could eat that much protein and fat first thing in the morning, and I'm just about to go for the eggs Benedict when I realise that I haven't actually eaten anything since yesterday lunchtime and I'm starving. I didn't even get to eat my cupcake.

'Do you know what?' I tell him. 'The full English sounds absolutely perfect.'

'The good news is that we're extremely unlikely to starve to death,' he tells me as he lights the burners and puts some sausages in the oven. 'Madame likes all the food to be as fresh as possible, but one day's worth of raw ingredients for fifty odd people will keep us going for ages. Do you want hash browns or fried bread?'

'I don't know. Which do you think is better?'

'The purist would argue that hash browns have no place in a full English, but I have to confess I prefer them to fried bread. You need some sort of carb to soak up the egg yolk though, so choose one.'

'Hash browns then, please.'

I watch as he pulls a bag out of one of the freezers and pops four hash browns onto a tray, before sliding it into the oven with the sausages.

'Do you think it's wrong, helping ourselves like this?' I ask.

'I wondered about that too, but most of this stuff is perishable. If we don't eat it, it'll only go in the bin. Plus, I think we can kiss any form of redundancy payout goodbye, so I don't feel bad about taking a bit of payment in kind. If we sold the entire wine cellar and pocketed the cash, that's one thing, but I don't think anyone would begrudge us having the odd glass of wine and eating food that will only go to waste otherwise.'

'Fair enough. Is there anything I can do?'

'I could murder a cappuccino.'

'It'll take a while. The machine needs half an hour to warm up after I've turned it on.'

'I'm not in any hurry. It's not as if I have a string of urgent appointments today.'

Although I've never used the barista machine at Hotel Dufour before, I'm familiar enough with how they work to operate it so, after checking that the water supply is turned on, I flip the switch and leave it to heat. Jock's remark about not having any appointments has brought back into focus something that has been bothering me.

'Jock?' I ask.

'Yes?'

'What are we going to do for the next week?'

'What do you mean?'

'I'll go mad with boredom sitting around here for a whole week. I'm used to being busy.'

'Hm. I hadn't thought that far ahead, but you're right. We're under curfew though, so we're kind of tied to the building.'

'Curfew, not house arrest. We're allowed out during the day, aren't we? As long as we're back by 7 p.m.'

'Good point.'

A plan is starting to form in my head. 'How well do you know London?'

'I can find my way about. The bus routes still confuse me sometimes.'

'I was thinking more about the tourist attractions.'

'Ah. I haven't visited any of them.'

'Me neither.'

'Really? But you've lived in London for ages, haven't you?'

'A few years, yes. But you know what it's like. Work is full on and days off are filled with boring chores like laundry and stuff. Plus, you tend to take the attractions for granted when they're on your front doorstep, don't you? So you think it's fine, you'll see them another day, but in reality, you never do. Also, these things aren't much fun on your own, are they?'

'Are you saying you don't have any friends down here to visit places with?'

'Do you?'

'No.'

'And probably for the same reason as me. But now we're stuck with each other for a whole week with nothing to do. So why don't we use the time to do a bit of sightseeing? It'll be a hell of a lot better than sitting around here all day, contemplating our fate and being miserable. Do you know, last night, before I came into your room, all I could think about was that going to prison would effectively end my career. This is all I've ever wanted, and the thought of losing it is almost worse than the idea of being locked up. I need things to distract me and keep that thought out of my head, so let's get out and about.'

He considers the thought for a moment before meeting my eyes and grinning. 'I think that's a brilliant idea.'

By the time breakfast is ready, I've drawn up a list of places we could go and start reading it to Jock.

'I've always wanted to go on the London Eye.'

'I'd be up for that.'

'Then there's the National Gallery and the National Portrait Gallery.'

'You're on your own for those, I'm afraid. Art isn't really my thing. Have you got the Tower of London on your list?'

'I have, but I'm not sure about it. Isn't it basically a prison? Feels a bit like tempting fate to me.'

'I don't think it was just a prison, and I've always wanted to see the crown jewels.'

'OK. Madame Tussauds?'

'Yes. Isn't the planetarium next door? We could do that at the same time.'

'Umm, I think that closed a while ago. Sorry.'

'Oh. Can we go to the Science Museum then?'

'I'm sensing a theme here. Only if we do the Natural History Museum as well.'

'Deal.'

The breakfast is absolutely delicious and, to my surprise, I eat it all. After we've cleared up, we carry our refilled coffee cups through to the bar and start to fill up a makeshift calendar with activities for each day until next Monday. We've got a real mix of stuff, from riding the Thames Clipper down to the Royal Observatory at Greenwich, through a picnic on Hampstead Heath, to attending a service at Westminster Abbey. I was a bit surprised when Jock suggested that one, but he pointed out that, not only would it do us good to get the Almighty on side in case we needed him, but it was also the only way to see inside the Abbey for free. To my amazement, he even begrudgingly agreed to visit the National Gallery with me in the end, although the Portrait Gallery is still hanging in the balance. We've checked the weather forecast and been online to make sure we don't plan activities at times when the attraction we're supposed to be visiting is shut. I've even found a store nearby where I can pick up a cheap digital camera to record our week in the absence of my phone, so I don't think we could be more organised if we tried.

We've decided to get the Almighty on side sooner rather than later, so we're going to go to Evensong this afternoon, but our first stop today is London Zoo. With a little bit of online sleuthing, I've worked out which buses we need to catch, both to get us to the zoo and also back to the Abbey in time for the service at five.

'I prefer the bus,' I'd explained to Jock when he'd expressed his worries that we might end up miles from our intended destination if we got it wrong. 'You don't see anything on the Tube, and it's so hot and stuffy down there.'

We've pre-booked our tickets for the zoo and, because neither of us have our phones, we've also printed off all the information we could possibly need to help us get the right buses, so I'm feeling optimistic as we step onto the pavement, locking the door behind us. We've barely covered five metres, however, when a man blocks our path.

'Hi there,' he says brightly, whipping his phone out to take a picture. 'Robin Bugg from the *Morning Post*. Can I ask you a few questions?'

Of course it was too good to be true. For a moment, I'm tempted to turn on my heel and flee back inside to safety, but there's no way I'm prepared to let some journalist deny me my freedom.

'*Lo siento, no hablo Ingles,*' I say as I grab Jock's hand and pull him past.

'I've no idea what she said,' Jock calls as we break into a run, 'but I'm going to guess she means fuck off.'

'What did you actually say?' he asks once we've slowed down, checked the journalist hasn't followed us and caught our breath. 'I'm not very good with languages, I'm afraid.'

'I told him in Spanish that I don't speak English. I couldn't think what else to do.'

'Impressive. Is that pretty much all of your vocabulary or are you fluent?'

'My mother is Spanish, so she brought me up speaking it at home.'

'That's so cool. If I had my time again, I'd definitely pay more attention to language classes at school.'

I'm still holding his hand as we make our way to the bus stop but, if he's noticed, he doesn't seem to mind. I'm surprised to find that I'm enjoying the sensation, and it makes us look like a normal couple appreciating the spring sunshine. Frankly, I'll take as much normality as I can right now, even if we're not a real couple. I'm delighted to see that the front seats on the upper deck of the bus are free when it arrives, so Jock and I grab them and enjoy the views of London as it picks its way through the traffic. Every time we arrive at a stop, I check it against the route plan that I've printed off, just to reassure us both that we're going the right way. The further away we get from the hotel, the more relaxed I start to feel and, at one point, I almost wonder if all the drama of yesterday was just a figment of my imagination. It wasn't, I know that, but it's lovely to be able to detach myself from it. I glance across at Jock and smile.

Today is going to be a good day.

6

'I feel incredibly peaceful,' I say quietly to Jock. The service has just finished and we're sitting in our seats soaking up the atmosphere of Westminster Abbey.

'I know what you mean,' he replies. 'I'm not especially religious, but there's something about being in a place like this and experiencing a ritual that's taken place, probably unchanged, for hundreds of years.'

'That piece they sang in the middle was so atmospheric. It sounds silly, but I actually felt quite emotional. What was it?'

He looks at the service sheet. '"Miserere" by Gregorio Allegri.'

'Are you two all right?' We look up to see one of the attendants gazing at us curiously. I'm sure there's a special name for whatever he is, but I have no idea what it is.

'Sorry, do we need to go?'

'We'll be locking up soon, but if you need some time for private prayer, I can come and get you in a few minutes.'

'No, it's fine, thank you. We were just saying how incredible the piece the choir sang in the middle of the service was.'

'The anthem? Yes, it's one of my favourites. It reminds us not only of our inherent sinfulness and wickedness, but more importantly of God's great mercy. There's a bit of a story attached to it, actually.'

'Go on,' I encourage him as we follow him towards the entrance.

'According to legend, it was only allowed to be performed in the Sistine Chapel and nobody outside the Vatican was permitted to see the sheet music. However, it escaped because Mozart heard it, memorised it and wrote it all down, which is why we're able to perform it today.'

'Is that true?'

'I doubt it, but it makes a good tale, doesn't it? You do need a capable choir to perform it though, because the soloist has to hit a top C, and there aren't that many people who can do it reliably.'

'I did notice the boy who did it getting looks from his colleagues.'

'Yes, I expect he'll be dining out on that for a while. Do you live locally?'

'It depends what you mean by local. We're in London, yes.'

'Well, do feel free to come anytime. We have Evensong every day. The times vary, but they're all published on our website.'

'Thank you, we might just do that.'

* * *

'I can't believe you got me to go to church and I enjoyed it,' I say to Jock as we make our way towards the bus stop.

'I did too. Although I don't think I'd want to do it every day, would you?'

'No. It would be like eating in a Michelin-starred restaurant every night; the magic would wear off pretty quickly. It needs to be a special occasion thing. Do you think God likes it? Or is he sitting up there on his cloud angrily shouting, "Change the tune!"'

'Maybe churches are like radio stations. He just tunes in to whichever one he's in the mood for.'

I smile. 'I like that idea.'

The bus is just leaving as we get to the stop and the board tells us there will be a fifteen-minute wait for the next one. Although it's still light, the heat has gone out of the day and I shiver in the cold breeze.

'Are you OK?' Jock asks. 'We could take the Tube if you'd rather. At least it will be warm.'

'No. I want to be outdoors. It sounds stupid, but I don't want to waste a moment of this week, and being underground feels wasteful.'

'Fair enough. I'd offer you my coat, but I don't have one. We could do the penguin thing, I guess.'

'What penguin thing?'

'I was reading about it while we were at the zoo. When male Emperor penguins are looking after the eggs, they all huddle together in a circle. The problem is, while that's lovely for the penguins in the middle, who are kept warm, it's not so much fun for the ones on the outside.'

'I can see that.'

'So they shuffle constantly in a kind of spiral, which means that everyone takes a turn on the outside but gets more time in the middle.'

'How does that apply to us?'

'Well, if I stand with my back to the breeze, you could stand in front of me and take shelter.'

'What, and then we swap over after a bit? I don't think I'm going to make a very good shelter for you, somehow.'

'You're right. It wasn't the best analogy, but I don't mind

staying on the outside. This is tropical weather compared to some of what I grew up with.'

Although we've spooned and held hands already today, they were both strictly accidental, to begin with at least. Consciously snuggling into his chest feels too intimate. However, I have to admit that the warmth coming off him as he wraps his arms around me and pulls me close is very welcome. After a moment's hesitation, I snake my arms around his back and squeeze him tight in return. I can feel myself relaxing as I breathe in the comforting scents of soap and fabric conditioner, and I can't help feeling a slight pang of disappointment when the bus finally arrives and he lets go so we can scramble aboard.

'You know what would make today absolutely perfect?' I ask him. The bus is crowded so we're having to stand, but I don't mind.

'No, what?'

'A glass of wine in a pub somewhere. Not just any old pub, but one overlooking a river, where we can sit outside because they've got those outdoor heaters.'

'That does sound nice, I agree. I don't think we have time before the curfew kicks in though.'

'I'd forgotten about that.'

'Yeah, it's a pain. Bloody curfew.'

'It's better than the alternative, I suppose.'

He sighs. 'You're right, but it's still a pity. The rest of the world is getting ready to kick back with a drink after a long day in the office, and we've got to skulk back to the hotel of shame, running the gauntlet of Robin bloody Bugg on the way.'

'Who?'

'The journalist from this morning. I'm pretty sure that's what he said his name was.'

'He's got to have lost interest by now, hasn't he?'

'We can hope. It's an unfortunate name for a journalist, isn't it?' he observes. 'Bugg – kind of implies he's squashable. I wouldn't mind squashing him. Maybe I will, if he's still there.'

'Yeah, I'm sure the police won't take a dim view of that at all,' I say, nudging him in the ribs.

'I'll threaten him with harassment then.'

'I'm not sure you can do that either, if it's in a public place. What a loathsome way to earn a living.'

'He probably thinks that about us, to be fair to the little rodent.'

'You have to choose. Rodent or bug, you can't have both.'

'And there, ladies and gentlemen, is the pedantic Beatrice we all know and love.'

'You're not funny.'

He grins. 'Only kidding. Oh, I think this is our stop.'

We're both on high alert as we make our way along the street to the rear entrance of the hotel, but thankfully there's no sign of the journalist, and we make it inside unmolested.

* * *

We're in the kitchen debating what to have for dinner when the rear door buzzer sounds again. The CCTV shows a uniformed policeman, and my heart is in my mouth as I hurry to open it. Has he come to take us back into custody? Maybe they've found some piece of incriminating evidence.

'Good evening, miss, sir,' he says officiously when I've let him in. 'Can I just check your names, for the record?'

'Beatrice Fairweather and Andrew McLaughlin,' Jock tells him.

'Excellent. Just checking you are where you're supposed to be. I'll leave you in peace. Have a good evening.'

'Are they going to check on us every day?' I ask Jock incredulously once the police officer has gone. I glance at the clock. 'It's only ten past seven. Talk about jobsworth.'

'I suspect it's a tactic. Check up on us the first day to make sure we behave for the rest of the week.'

'Well, he's certainly put a dampener on my mood. I was just about to say how much I've enjoyed myself today, but now all I can think about is the fact that we're not free. Not properly, anyway.'

He comes over and pulls me into another hug. 'Don't let him spoil it. He was just doing his job and he's gone now. Don't think about him; think about the good things. Think about the sloth, and the "Miserere" in the Abbey.'

'I did like the sloth,' I say to his chest as I secretly soak up the pleasure of being in his arms again. I'm not normally a particularly physical person, but then this isn't a particularly normal week.

'Did you know that a sloth's internal organs are stuck to its ribcage to make it easier for it to breathe when hanging upside down?'

'Where do you learn that?'

'It was on the sign next to the enclosure. Pretty cool, huh? Apparently, they have so little spare energy because of their diet that trying to breathe against the weight of their internal organs would exhaust them otherwise.'

I pull away and look up at him. 'Who needs David Attenborough when I've got you, eh?'

'I do what I can. Now, dinner. We've got loads of prawns, so I could make a prawn cocktail to start if you're feeling retro, or I could do them with garlic, chilli and lemon if you prefer.'

'What's prawn cocktail in French?'

'No idea. It was the one retro dish Madame hated, so I was never allowed to put it on the menu.'

'Let's have that then, just to piss her off.'

He smiles. 'OK. Fish, meat or vegetarian main?'

'*Canard à l'orange*?' I suggest.

'No. I've got oranges but no duck. If you're very good, I'll do you *crêpes suzettes* for pudding. How's that?'

'Ooh. Will you bring the trolley and flambé them at the table like you did for the guests?'

'No, because I always felt incredibly self-conscious doing that and, frankly, it's naff.'

'And prawn cocktail isn't?'

He sighs. 'Do you really want them flambéed at the table?'

'I know you'll probably think less of me, but I kind of do. I've never been to a restaurant where someone has flambéed something at the table for me.'

He laughs. 'Where have you hidden this side of your character? The Beatrice I thought I knew would never get excited about something like that. She'd be far too busy checking that the napkins were perfectly ironed.'

I open my mouth to challenge him, before realising that he's probably right. 'Attention to detail matters,' I tell him defensively instead.

'Of course it does. Sorry, I didn't mean to upset you.'

'I'm not upset, but it must be the same for you, surely? You wouldn't send something out if you weren't a hundred per cent happy with it, would you? Even if it's only a sodding potato croquette.'

He holds up his hands in surrender. 'Fine. We're both obsessive about our work. Anyway, your wish is my command and I will flambé for you. Now, mains. I've got steak, chicken, some nice halibut or wild mushroom tortellini.'

'If we had steak, I could open a bottle of the South African Pinotage to go with it. How big are they?'

'Various sizes. Madame liked to sell them by the hundred gram; she thought that gave them a "fresh from the market" vibe.'

'I'll have a small one. Have you got any of those matchstick fries?'

'*Pommes de terre frites à la julienne*? Yes, I think so.'

'Let's have some of those as well then. Do you need a hand?'

'Yes, you can do the prawn cocktail. The prawns are in the fridge, and you'll want iceberg lettuce as well. For the sauce, you need mayonnaise, tomato ketchup, a lemon, Worcester sauce and a pinch of paprika. The mayo is your base; just add the others until it tastes right.'

'Ketchup?'

'Yup. I'm pretty sure that's why Madame banned it. She thought ketchup was for tradespeople.'

Twenty minutes later, the steaks are resting and we carry our prawn cocktails into the dining room, where I've laid a table for two and lit a candle. I've opened the Pinotage and Jock pours us both generous glasses once we've sat down.

'Cheers!' Jock clinks his glass against mine, and I can't help noticing the twinkle of his eyes in the candlelight.

The conversation flows easily as we make our way through the food we've prepared, no doubt helped by the generous measures of wine. Jock is as good as his word, bringing the crêpes over on the trolley and flambéing them at the table. Every gesture is given added theatre – a flourish here, a flamboyant pour of the Grand Marnier there – and I can't help but laugh at how over-the-top it all is. I'm surprised to see that we've managed to polish off the bottle of wine between us. Although I feel very mellow, I don't feel tipsy at all so, after we've washed up, I accept Jock's invitation to a nightcap in the bar.

'Thank you,' I say as I rest my head on his shoulder.

'What for?'

'For today. For cheering me up after the policeman came. For your frankly ludicrous flambé. For all of it.'

'Ah, you're more than welcome. It was fun, wasn't it? And tomorrow, we'll have another set of adventures. This was a very good idea of yours.'

I yawn. 'It wasn't bad, was it?'

I feel pleasantly full and sleepy as we climb the stairs to bed, but that doesn't stop a niggle of anxiety forming in the pit of my stomach as I contemplate a repeat of last night's failed attempt to get to sleep.

'Are you going to be all right?' Jock asks when we reach our rooms. 'Or do you want to stay with me again tonight?'

'I'm sure I'll be fine. I don't want to impose.'

'Hey, it's no skin off my nose. Who knows, we might get closer to finding out which of us is the phantom spooner.'

It's not much of a dilemma. 'Give me ten minutes to change, brush my teeth and grab my pillow,' I tell him.

He smiles. 'I'll be waiting.'

7

It's Sunday evening and we're celebrating the end of our sightseeing adventure with a traditional roast dinner. I say traditional, but we've had to adapt it slightly to fit with the ingredients we've got available. Madame didn't believe in roast dinners so we haven't got a joint anywhere, but we do have some poussins, which were on the menu as *Poussin à la Provençale*, so we're going to roast a couple of those and have them with all the trimmings. Jock has put me to work on making the bread sauce and preparing the pigs in blankets by cutting sausages in half and wrapping thin strips of bacon round them.

'Which was your favourite activity this week?' I ask him.

'I enjoyed all of them, really. Well, that's not quite true. I could take or leave the National Gallery, but I liked seeing how much pleasure it gave you. The picnic was fun. Hampstead Heath is such an iconic location, isn't it? It felt like we were in a romcom, and Hugh Grant was going to appear at any moment. What about you?'

'How could I not say the picnic, when you went to so much trouble with the food?'

'It was nothing.'

'I'm never going to be able to eat a supermarket scotch egg again, having tasted the ones you made.'

'I can't believe how much I've enjoyed cooking this week. It's been such a relief to cook the food I love and not be tied to Madame's stuffy ideas.'

He's right. After our homage to the seventies on Tuesday night, Jock changed tack and we've been eating much lighter, more modern fare on the whole. He managed to offload some of the perishable goods to a homeless charity he found on the internet so, despite the fact that our own consumption has barely made a dent in the mountain of food, we haven't had to throw very much away.

The police haven't bothered to check up on us again so, apart from the odd moment when the reality of our situation has caused a knot to form in the pit of my stomach, we've been able to more or less pretend that we're on holiday.

'If I say something cheesy, will you promise not to laugh?' I ask as we settle ourselves at the table and Jock pours the wine.

'What level of cheese are we talking? If it's a light dusting of parmesan, I reckon I can keep a straight face. If you're going full-on baked camembert, I can't promise anything.'

'It's probably somewhere in between the two.'

'I'll do my best to contain myself then.'

'I was just going to say that I can't think of anyone I would rather have spent this week with than you. Thank you.' I raise my glass and chink it against his.

To my surprise, he blushes. 'I've really enjoyed it too,' he says quietly.

I've never felt this connected to anyone after just a few days in their company. I know we've been colleagues since I arrived here, but I've only really got to know Jock properly this week. I think the only time we haven't been together is when we've been getting dressed in the morning or getting ready for bed. Normally, I'd be feeling a bit stifled if I had to spend that much time with one person, but spending time with Jock is easy. We've talked about all kinds of things; he's told me about his parents and his older brother Fergus, who moved to Tuscany to open a retreat centre with the love of his life, Alberto. In return, I've given him the lowdown on my experiences growing up as the only child of hotel owners in Ludlow. I haven't spoken to Mum since Monday but she won't think that's odd. We can often go months without speaking. I'm also still irritated by her volte-face about me coming home, even though I had no intention of taking her up on her original invitation.

'Are you OK there?' Jock asks. 'You look like you popped out for a moment.'

'Sorry, I was just thinking about what my mother said.'

'Will you call her tomorrow, once you get your phone back?'

'*If* I get my phone back. It's doubtful; she probably hasn't given me another thought.'

'I'm sure she has,' he says encouragingly.

'Have you told your parents? About being arrested, I mean.'

'God, no! My mother would have been on the first plane or train down here; she'd have gone straight to the police station and given them absolute hell for daring to believe that her son could be mixed up in something like this. Then she'd have come here and ripped into me for not spotting what Madame was up to. I love my mum, but she's not someone you mess with.'

'I think I'd rather have that than "Please stay away because we don't want to be associated with you right now".'

'She is quite protective of us. It's funny because I remember Fergus being really anxious about telling her he was gay. She didn't give a hoot about that, but she must have grilled poor Alberto for hours before she pronounced him worthy of her boy.'

'What about your dad? How did he feel?'

Jock grins. 'Dad would have felt exactly how Mum told him to feel. He knows better than to cross her.'

A thought occurs to me. 'Wouldn't she have seen you on the news?'

'I'd know if she had.'

'How? She can't get hold of you on your mobile because the police have it, and she wouldn't be able to get through on the hotel phone either because it's off the hook.'

'Is she here?'

'No.'

'Then she doesn't know. Pudding?'

'Please.'

Jock tops up our glasses before taking the plates out to the kitchen, returning a minute or so later with two ramekins.

'It's the leftover lemon possets from the picnic,' he explains as he puts one down in front of me. 'I cut the recipe down as much as I could, but you can't really do fewer than four as a minimum.'

'That's OK.' I smile. 'I'm more than happy to have it again. You've completely spoiled me, you realise that? I'm never going to be able to have half the things I like again without remembering the way you made them.'

'I'm glad I've made an impression.' He laughs.

'God, this is good,' I groan as I take a mouthful. 'You've basically ruined all lemon-flavoured desserts for ever.'

'It's OK,' he admits. 'I wouldn't call it life-changing though.'

'If I go to prison tomorrow, I want to remember this flavour. In fact, never mind the drugs and all the other stuff you can get smuggled into prisons; I'd be happy with contraband lemon posset once a week.'

'That might be difficult.'

'Why?'

'If they've found enough to convict you, then I'll be in prison as well. Who will you get to make it? Anyway, we're not going to prison, so you don't need to worry about it.'

'Are you sure?'

'We haven't done anything wrong. You need to hold on to that, Beatrice. How can they find evidence to convict you if you haven't broken the law? This isn't some banana republic where they just lock you up anyway. They have to prove you're guilty, remember?'

'You're right. I know you're right, but I still have these wobbles from time to time. I do try to imagine putting all this behind me and getting my life back on track, but it's hard.'

'That's normal. I have wobbles too. The trick is not to let them take hold. Think of it this way: by this time tomorrow, it will all be over.'

I sigh. 'I wish I could look at it like that. All I can think about is that this might be my last night of freedom. Tonight: roast chicken, lemon posset and wine. Tomorrow: prison uniform, gruel, dry bread and water with a dead cockroach in it.'

He laughs. 'I think you'll find things have moved on since the Victorian era.'

'Yeah, but one thing hasn't. If we go to prison, that's a criminal record and nobody will ever hire us again. I love this job, Jock. I can't even think about doing something else.'

'That's true but, as I keep saying, it's not going to go that way. Here's the deal. I will meet you in the bar at seven tomorrow night. Wear your best dress because we're going to be celebrating. How does that sound?'

I sigh. 'Fine. If we're cleared tomorrow, I'll be here. What if it's neither?'

'What do you mean?'

'I just thought. They don't have to convict or release. They could keep us on bail for another week.'

'If they do that, I'm sure we can find more sights to see.'

'How do you do it?'

'What?'

'Remain so positive about everything.'

'The way I look at life is this. There are things I can control and things I can't. There's no point in worrying about the things I can control, because I should be able to change them if I don't like them. Equally, there's no point in worrying about the things I can't control, because there's nothing I can do to influence the outcome. Tell me something: do you worry about dying?'

'OK, that's not where I was expecting this to go. Bit dark, Jock.'

'I'm not trying to be depressing; I'm just making a point. Do you?'

'It's not something I think about, no.'

'But you could die tomorrow. You might get run over by a bus, or shot by a terrorist, or a piano might fall on your head. Equally, you might live until you're 103 and die peacefully at home surrounded by your great grandchildren. You can't control it, so why worry about it? Do you see where I'm coming from?'

'I guess so. You could have picked a different analogy though.'

'It's a good one for this. So, you might die tomorrow or you might not. You might go to prison tomorrow or you might not. You have no control over either of those things, so don't waste time stressing about them.'

'Ah, but that's where your analogy falls down.'

'How?'

'If I don't die tomorrow then it will just be another day, because I'm not expecting to die. But I'm definitely going to the police station, and *something* is going to happen one way or another. It's an actual event that could have life-changing consequences, and therefore I'm worried about it.' I think for a moment. 'A better analogy would be waiting for the results of a biopsy. It might be benign, or it might be malignant, but it's going to have a big impact either way.'

'Ah well. I tried. But I don't think it hurts to be optimistic.'

'I'm not so sure. Haven't you ever heard the proverb?'

'Which one?'

'Blessed are the pessimists, for they shall never be disappointed.'

He laughs, and the sound of it fills the empty room.

'I'll have to remember that one for Fergus. He'll love it. Shall we clear up and have a nightcap before bed?'

'You're a terrible influence on me. I don't think I've ever drunk as much as I have this week.'

'Me neither, but we're on holiday, aren't we?'

* * *

It's accepted now that I'll be spending the night in Jock's room, and I no longer bother to remove my pillow each morning. We've also given up trying to work out which of us is the phantom spooner; as soon as we're both in bed, I nestle into him and he puts his arm around me. Normally, I'm asleep within minutes, but I can't stop my brain churning tonight.

'I can hear you,' Jock murmurs sleepily.

'What?'

'You're thinking. I can hear the cogs in your head.'

I roll over to face him. He hasn't moved his arm, so our noses are practically touching.

'I'm scared, Jock. I've tried the not-worrying-about-stuff-I-can't-control thing, but it's not working. What if I go to prison tomorrow for a really long time? I'll never see the things I want to see, do the things I want to do, love the people I want to love.'

He brings his hand up and strokes my cheek. 'You will do all of those things.'

He's so close that I can't focus on him, but I don't need to. Something powerful is stirring deep inside me, and I'm both energised and terrified by it.

'Jock?' I whisper.

'Yes?'

'Do you think I'm attractive?'

His eyes snap open. 'Is that a trick question?'

'No.'

'Of course I do. You're beautiful. Why?'

'Kiss me.'

'What?'

'I've realised that you're right. I can't control what happens to me tomorrow, but I need to seize everything today. I want to feel alive. I want to feel powerful. I want to feel desired. I want...' I tail off.

He stares at me for the longest time without moving and I'm on the verge of fleeing to my room in humiliation when he inches forwards until his lips brush against mine. We lie there for what feels like an age, our lips just touching, and I can feel the heat building up inside me until I'm fizzing. Just when I think I can't take any more, he pulls me against him and deepens the kiss, lifting my sleep shirt and slipping his hand underneath. I sigh with pleasure at the sensation. There is no doubt where this is going and, although a tiny part of me questions the wisdom of it, given that we'll be separated in a day or two whatever happens tomorrow, I want this. In fact, it's more primitive than that; I need this.

8

Having sex with Jock turned out to be just the tonic I needed, and I slept soundly until he woke me at seven thirty. I was initially anxious that he might have regretted it and there would be an awkward atmosphere, but he obviously sensed my unease as he held me for a long time and told me it had felt like the most natural thing in the world. I agreed, and we ended up doing it again. Despite a good night's rest and the endorphins that are probably still floating around my body, my heart is in my mouth as we leave the hotel to make our way to the custody centre where we will learn our fate. Having studied the Tube and bus routes, we agreed a taxi would be the most reliable option, and I'm drinking in the view as it trundles along, just in case this is my final glimpse of freedom. I feel like I might throw up at any minute. We've given ourselves plenty of time; better to be early than late for something like this. I wonder how long they give you before they decide you're a no-show and issue a warrant for your arrest. Ten minutes? A couple of hours?

I'm shivering with nerves when the taxi pulls up outside, and Jock has to help me out as my legs are feeling so wobbly. He's trying to appear relaxed, but I can feel the tension radiating off him. Underneath the façade, he's just as scared as me.

There's a different custody officer on the desk today, and he looks at us quizzically as we make our way through the door.

'Can I help you?' he asks.

'Andrew McLaughlin and Beatrice Fairhead,' Jock tells him. 'We have a bail appointment at ten o'clock.'

The officer glances at the clock behind him. 'You're a bit early, it's only nine thirty. Did you want to wait or come back?'

Jock looks at me. 'Wait,' I whisper. Now I'm here, I can't stomach the idea of going away for half an hour. What would we do? Sitting quietly in a chair is probably the best thing for me right now.

'Fine,' the custody officer says. 'Take a seat and I'll let them know you're here.'

By ten fifteen, I'm in total meltdown and wondering if this is some kind of mad power game they like to play. Make you wait longer, just to soften you up before they deliver the fatal blow. It's working; I'd probably be prepared to confess to pretty much anything, just to end the waiting. I'm sure the clock has been running deliberately slowly, as this is by far the longest forty-five minutes of my life. At one point, my teeth started chattering and Jock took my hand in his in an attempt to reassure me. I've been hanging on to it like grim death ever since, even though both our hands are sweaty and it's not actually that pleasant a sensation.

At twenty-five past, the door finally opens and DS Hollis appears, along with another detective I don't recognise.

'Beatrice, you're with me,' he announces. 'Andrew, I think you know my colleague DS Harvey.'

'Good luck,' Jock murmurs to me, planting a kiss on my forehead as he lets go of my hand and gets to his feet. It takes all my willpower to force my legs into action and get out of the seat, and

I follow DS Hollis unsteadily to the same interview room I was in last week.

'Take a seat,' DS Hollis instructs, holding the door open. 'We'll be with you in just a minute.'

The click of the door closing and the lock engaging sound so final that, before I know it, the tears are pouring down my cheeks. This is it, the beginning of my incarceration, I just know it. I may be innocent, but that doesn't mean anything in here. You hear about people who serve years and years before they manage to clear their name, and they made it very obvious that they didn't believe a word of my story last time I was here. This whole week has just been a cruel game, I realise. It's like when a cat catches a mouse. It lets the mouse think it's escaped before pouncing again and again until the mouse is dead. That's what the police have done to me, and I almost wish they'd kept me in custody rather than let me hope like I have been. I'm full-on sobbing now, and I can feel a river of snot running onto my top lip.

'Sorry to keep you,' DI Winter says as she and DS Hollis re-enter the room. 'You have no idea how much paperwork we have to fill in. Goodness, are you all right?'

'Sorry,' I sniff.

'DS Hollis, fetch a box of tissues, will you?' DI Winter instructs. 'And some sweet tea.'

'It's fine,' I tell her. 'Let's just get this over with.'

'Are you sure?'

Her kindness doesn't fool me. What's the point of tea and tissues now, when the van is probably already outside, waiting to take me to prison?

'Yes,' I tell her.

'Fine.' She plonks a large file stuffed with papers onto the table between us, and she and DS Hollis sit down opposite me.

'So, the good news is that we have concluded our investigations, as far as you are concerned anyway. We have consulted with the Crown Prosecution Service, and they agree that there aren't sufficient grounds to formally charge you with an offence.'

'I'm sorry? What does that mean?'

'It means we won't be taking this any further and you're free to go. Do you have any questions?'

I can't make sense of this at all. I was so convinced that I was going to prison that my mind just doesn't seem to be able to comprehend the fact that I'm not.

'How? Last week, you said you didn't believe me.'

'You're right. There were a number of aspects of your story that didn't make sense in isolation. However, when we combine it with the other evidence we've gathered, it actually checks out.'

'What other evidence?'

'I'm afraid that's confidential. What I can tell you is that we've learned that you were deliberately kept in the dark. It was important that the hotel appeared respectable, on the surface at least. That's what your role was.'

'Did Madame tell you that?'

'Eileen?' DS Hollis laughs. 'She may be a slip of a thing, but she's tough as nails, that one. She's not giving anything away.'

'Thank you, DS Hollis.' DI Winter's tone is disapproving and I briefly wonder if she has to tell him off a lot.

'So Madame – Eileen – is she going to prison?'

'That will depend on whether we put forward enough evidence for a jury to convict her. Is there anything pertinent to your own case that you'd like to know before you leave?'

'Can I have my phone back?'

'Absolutely. As soon as we're finished here, DS Hollis will escort you back to the desk, and the custody officer will return it. Anything else?'

'No. Not that I can think of.'

'Great. Thank you for being so co-operative, Beatrice, and I'm sorry you had to go through this.' She picks up the folder of papers and gets to her feet. 'There's a toilet by the front door if you need to sort yourself out a bit once the paperwork is complete. Oh, and I'm going to give you my card. If you need to speak to me for any reason, it has the number of my direct line.'

I take the card she's holding out and put it in my purse, although I can't think what would make me want to call her. I'm still trying to process what they've said as I follow DS Hollis back through the door to the desk. How can something as enormous as telling me I'm a free woman be made to feel so mundane?

When we get to the desk, I'm relieved to see that Jock is already there, waiting for me. My hands are still shaking as I sign the forms and the custody officer hands my phone back. I try to turn it on, but there's no charge, unsurprisingly.

'What happened to you?' Jock asks, his voice full of concern.

'What do you mean?'

'You look like you've just stepped out of a boxing ring.'

'He's not wrong,' the custody officer agrees. 'Toilets are just behind you if you need them.'

I don't really want to go into the toilets. I want to go through the front door and get as far away from here as I possibly can, but the look of concern on both men's faces convinces me that I ought to take a look at least. As soon as I catch a glimpse of my face in the mirror, I can see what they mean. My eyes are red and puffy from crying; my face is blotchy and there's a nasty shiny track from my nose down to my mouth. I turn on the cold tap and splash my face with water to try to get rid of the worst of it. By the time I'm done, I'm still no portrait, but I'm unlikely to frighten children in the street.

'I've called a taxi,' Jock tells me when I reappear. 'It should be here in ten minutes or so.'

'Great. Can we wait outside?'

'Of course.'

'What happened?' Jock asks again once we're through the door and out of earshot of the police.

'I had a bit of a meltdown when they shut me in the interview room,' I explain.

He pulls me into a tight hug and kisses the top of my head. 'It's over, Beatrice,' he says. 'We're free.'

I'm still trying to process that information as we head back to the hotel. He's right. It's over, and I can start planning for the future again. I feel light-headed with relief as the taxi pulls up outside the back door and we clamber out.

'I've got a few things I need to sort out,' Jock tells me once we're inside. 'I'll see you in the bar at seven, OK?'

'What?'

'Don't tell me you've forgotten. Our celebration.'

'Oh yes. Sorry. Best dress.'

'I've been thinking about that and I've decided to make a change. Dress warmly instead.'

'How formal?'

'Jeans and hoodie are fine, but make sure you've got a coat. We're going to be outdoors.'

As soon as I get into my room, I plug my phone in to charge before sitting on the bed and reflecting on everything that's happened in the last week. I'm free. It's over. On the one hand, I'm ecstatic, obviously. I can start looking for work and get my life back on track. But I can't deny I'm going to miss the little bubble that Jock and I have been in since we were arrested. We've both been up front about the fact that this was never going to turn into anything more, that we'd be going our separate ways, but part of me can't help wishing that it could have been something more. I'm going to miss him, that's for sure. But we've got to be realistic;

we both need jobs and the probability of finding a hotel that needs both a head chef and a manager is non-existent.

To distract myself from thinking about Jock, I let my eyes wander round the room that's been my home since I started at Hotel Dufour. I haven't really spent any time in here since my arrest, but sitting in here now reminds me that other people, people I don't know, have been in this room going through my stuff. I consider my options as I lay back on my bed. I decide to have a purge and get rid of everything that reminds me of Madame (the black skirts and jackets, plus the white blouses), and replace all my underwear. People rifling through my jeans and tops I can cope with. Rummaging through my knickers and bras, no.

I grab a couple of bin bags from the communal kitchen and start stuffing clothes into them. By the time I'm done, my wardrobe is looking surprisingly bare, but I feel much better. Two hours later, my bra and knicker drawers are refreshed with the new underwear I've bought, I've changed what I'm wearing and all of the unwanted clothes have either been donated to charity or binned. My phone is now fully charged, so I turn it on.

At first glance, I haven't missed much. There are the text and voicemail messages I was expecting from Mum on the day I was arrested, plus some missed calls from unfamiliar numbers that I'm guessing were probably journalists. However, I'm bombarded with notifications from my normally silent social media feeds, and I quickly discover they're all from people checking in to see if I'm OK. It's a nice feeling to know that people have been worried about me; since moving to London, I've been so immersed in my work that, not only have I not made any friends down here, I also haven't really kept in regular contact with people I was close to at home and uni. I seize the opportunity to catch up with a few of them, passing several hours very happily. I even managed to have a reasonably constructive conversation with my parents, inasmuch as they agreed to let me stay with them while I search for a new job. I'm certain I want to look for another post in London, but there's no way I can afford to stay here while I'm officially unemployed. Also, although you could never accuse me of suffering from lack of motivation, being under the same roof as Mum and Dad is going to seriously focus my mind on finding a new position.

I'm aware of Jock returning late in the afternoon but, now that we're no longer tied together by our bail conditions and we're about to go our separate ways, I feel a little unsure about how I'm supposed to act with him. Yes, we've had sex twice, but maybe they were just acts of desperation between two frightened people. The fact remains that our destinies are different, this has just been a refuge for us both when we needed it, and I know I need to let him go. Despite that, I feel a pang of sadness that this will be our last night together, and I'm in a reflective mood when we meet in the bar at seven.

'Are you OK?' Jock asks as the taxi trundles west. 'You're very quiet.'

'Sorry. Just trying to make sense of everything, I suppose.'

He smiles. 'Dare I suggest you're overthinking again?'

'You're right,' I sigh. 'Sorry. Tell me where we're going.'

'It's a surprise, but it's not far now.'

Sure enough, the taxi turns into a pub car park a few minutes later.

'Long way to come for a pub, Jock,' I remark as we climb out and he pays the driver.

'It's not just any pub. Come on.'

He leads me inside and gives his name at the welcome desk. With a smile, the waiter takes us through the dining room and onto a terrace, where I suddenly realise what he's done.

'Outdoor heaters and a river.' I sigh contentedly.

'My original plan was to go somewhere incredibly upmarket to celebrate. Somewhere that does the kind of food I want to cook. But then I thought about your remark on the bus the other day and I realised you would enjoy this much more. Is it all right?'

'It's more than all right,' I tell him, leaning across to give him a kiss. 'It's perfect.'

9

I don't think I could be any more content. I've got a cold glass of Chablis and, even though it's dark and the temperature has dropped, I'm perfectly warm thanks to the patio heaters out here. Beyond the terrace, I can hear faint sounds from the river below. Jock is patiently letting me take it all in, not crowding me with chatter.

'Where did you learn to be so good at reading women?' I ask after a while.

'I'm not sure I am.'

'I disagree. I would have been a complete basket case this last week if it hadn't been for you. You appear to know how to calm me and reassure me, without resorting to annoying platitudes. Even last night and this morning, you just seemed to be in tune with what I needed.'

He smiles. 'You were fairly direct. It wasn't hard to follow, as instructions go.'

I can feel the heat in my cheeks, and I avert my gaze to take a sip of wine while I try to regain my composure. Although I have no regrets about what we did, I do need to let him know that he doesn't owe me anything. I'd hate him to feel tied to me, just because of a few moments of shared intimacy.

'I don't want what happened to change anything between you and me,' I say eventually.

Something flashes across his eyes, but it's too fast for me to read. 'Really?' he says. 'You could have told me before I spent the entire afternoon looking at possible wedding venues.'

'Oh, God. Jock, I'm so sorry...' I begin, but I'm cut off by his laughter.

'I had you going properly there, didn't I?'

'You know all those nice things I said about you just now? I take them all back. You're a bastard.'

He smiles. 'It's fine. I know we're time limited. Thinking of which, what are you going to do now?'

'I spoke to my parents and I'm going to head home tomorrow. You?'

'I had a chat with my mum which went pretty much as I predicted. Ideally, I'd give her a week or so to cool off, but I need somewhere to stay while I look for work, so I'm going to do the same.'

Our conversation is interrupted by the arrival of our starters. We've both gone for fish, with whitebait for Jock and calamari for me. I'm not normally a fan of whitebait, but Jock tells me they're among the best he's had, so I accept his offer to try one and I have to admit that it's good. I'm less impressed when he seizes a piece of my calamari in return.

'What's your dream?' I ask him once the starters have been cleared away.

'Same as every chef, probably. I want my own restaurant. My name above the door.'

'*Chez* Jock?'

He laughs. 'I can tell you right now that there will be no

bloody French, either in the name or on the menu. Madame has put me off that for life.'

'Why don't you, then?'

'Why don't I what?'

'Go out on your own.'

'Money, mainly. I've got a fair amount saved from my time at Hotel Dufour but nowhere near enough that a bank would come near me. Plus, it's a lovely dream, but do you know how many restaurants fail?'

'No. How many?'

'Sixty per cent fold within the first year alone.'

'Wow, that's massive.'

'It gets worse. Eighty per cent fail within five years. Not great odds, are they?'

'But you're good. Even when you were tied to Madame's menu, the dining room was still full pretty much every night. The stuff you've been cooking this week has been next level, so I'm sure they'd come flocking.'

'Two problems there. The food is just a tiny part of what it takes to make a restaurant successful, and the dining room was full because I suspect most of our guests didn't want to waste time going out to eat when there were such compelling reasons to be in their rooms.'

'I'll accept the second one, but surely a restaurant is all about the food.'

'Food is important, certainly. But so is the location, the concept, getting the prices right and so on. You could be producing the most amazing dishes, but you're going to go out of business pretty quickly if nobody can find you, or it's horribly overpriced, or there are three other restaurants within half a mile doing the same thing.'

'Your dream sounds kind of depressing,' I observe.

'I wouldn't call it depressing so much as difficult. I'm still going to try to do it one day. I'm an optimist, as you know, so I'm always going to believe I will succeed where others have failed. What about you? What's your dream?'

'Easy. My own hotel.'

'Off you go then.'

'If only. You need serious capital behind you, not my paltry savings.'

'What would it look like?'

'It would be a country house hotel, set in its own grounds. An old manor house or something like that; somewhere with lots of charm and character.'

'Really? I thought you'd go modern.'

'No. Modern hotels are too soulless. I'd have modern touches, of course. Power showers with rainfall heads, fluffy bathrobes and duvets on the beds, but there would also be open fireplaces in the lounges and oak panelling scattered about. There would be flower arrangements using flowers from the garden, and wellies in every size by the front door so guests could explore outdoors without getting their shoes muddy.'

'Wow. That's very specific.'

'Yeah, but what's the point of dreams if you don't indulge every fantasy? I know it's not going to happen, but it's a nice way to drift off to sleep sometimes. Don't tell me you don't do it.'

He grins. 'I might.'

We're silent again as we eat our main courses. Jock has ordered a burger because, according to him, he hasn't had one for ages and really craved it, and I've gone for lasagne. Jock raises his eyebrows when I ask for some Worcestershire sauce to go with it.

'What?' I ask him.

'Mixing your cultures there a bit, aren't you?'

'Are you honestly telling me you've never had Worcester sauce with lasagne? It's one of the greats, like brown sauce and bacon, or chips and egg.'

He looks decidedly sceptical so, when the server brings the bottle, I add a generous amount to my dish and offer him a forkful. He eyes it suspiciously for a moment, as if I might be trying to poison him, before allowing me to put it into his mouth. His face puckers in disgust straightaway, and then relaxes.

'Do you know what?' he says. 'That's actually not bad.'

'Praise indeed.' I laugh.

'It's still wrong, of course, but I can see why you like it.'

'It can't be wrong if it tastes good. Give us a chip.'

'As long as you don't do anything weird with it, like dip it in orange squash or something.'

'There isn't any squash here, so I'll have to slum it with tradespeople's ketchup.' I deliberately take the largest chip off his plate and make a show of dipping it in his pot of ketchup, staring provocatively into his eyes as I bite into it.

'Don't think that's going back in the ketchup after you've chewed it,' he warns me softly.

'Perish the thought,' I say coquettishly, before lunging at the pot of ketchup with the chip. He's too quick for me though, and he scoops it safely out of my reach.

'Nice try.' He smiles as I pout sulkily and shove the rest of the chip in my mouth. This proves to be a mistake, as it's still ferociously hot so I end up sort of panting, trying to cool it down without spitting it out. Jock bursts out laughing.

'The thing I like about you, Beatrice, is that you're always so ladylike,' he says through his guffaws.

'Piss off,' I tell him. Unfortunately, my mouth is still full of the chip, so it comes out more like 'Pith off', which only makes him laugh harder.

* * *

The kitchen buzzer sounds the next morning while we're preparing breakfast, making us both jump. We're both still in our dressing gowns, having had sex again before coming down. Jock is cooking a light breakfast of scrambled eggs and bacon while I'm carefully making two cappuccinos, making sure I'm well out of the way of any sudden bursts of steam from the machine. Neither of us are talking about our imminent separation, but it's hanging in the air.

'What the bloody hell?' Jock murmurs as he looks at the CCTV feed.

'Who is it?' I ask.

'Maria.'

He doesn't get time to elaborate, because the buzzing is now accompanied by a furious banging on the door.

'All right, I'm coming. Keep your hair on,' Jock mutters as he makes his way over to open the door.

'You took your time,' Maria spits as soon as he lets her in. Her expression is hostile as she casts her eyes over the kitchen. 'What's going on here?'

'We're just making breakfast. Do you want some?'

'I hope you're paying for it,' she retorts. 'I'd hate to think you've been taking *advantage* of poor Madame's situation.'

'How are you, Maria?' I ask, somewhat disconcerted by her attitude, which is even more unpleasant than usual.

'Oh, I'm just peachy thanks. You know, having spent a week in police custody and all.'

'I thought they had to release you within a certain time?'

'They do, but the initial condition was that I couldn't live here, and I had nowhere else to go, so it took a shitload of time for my brief to sort it all out.'

'But they've let you go now. That's a good sign, isn't it?'

'Only if the lawyer does his job right and makes sure I don't get a custodial sentence. Bloody pigs. They ought to be out catching murderers, rather than coming after people like us who are simply providing a service.'

'It was illegal, Maria.'

'Don't come all high and mighty with me, Beatrice. You should be thanking me.'

'Why?'

'Who do you think told the police you didn't know anything about it, eh? If it wasn't for me, you might still be in there, so a little gratitude wouldn't go amiss, frankly.'

'Thank you.'

'That's better. Right, I'm taking charge as of now. We've got a lot to do before we reopen.'

'Sorry,' I say gently. 'I'm not sure I heard you right. You're reopening?'

'Of course we are. We're losing money hand over fist every day we're closed. We'll have to change the business model a little, but that's not the end of the world.'

'You mean, operate purely as a hotel?' I ask hopefully. Maybe that wouldn't be too bad, although I don't like the idea of working for Maria at all. However, it would give me somewhere in London to live and an income while I look for something else.

'Don't be daft. We'll never make any money that way. We'll still offer extras but, rather than using our own in-house resource, we'll have to make arrangements with some local providers I know. It won't be as profitable, and we'll need a bit of a rebrand to keep the police out of our faces, but we were always ready for this.'

'What?' Jock looks up from the two plates he's just placed our breakfast on. 'Are you telling me you *planned* for this?'

'Naturally. You don't go into this business without a plan B.'

'And what was yours?' I ask. I'm fascinated and horrified by her in equal measure.

'Simple. Madame takes the hit. She was always going to get custodial with her history, so it made sense. I throw myself on the mercy of the pigs and sell her down the river in the hope of getting non-custodial. I then look after her business interests until she's released and everything goes back to normal.'

'It's a lot of trust to put in you,' I observe. 'You must be really close.'

'Of course we are,' she states as if I'm stupid. 'She's my mum.'

Of all the things I expected Maria to say, that one never crossed my mind, and I think my mouth might be open in surprise.

'She's your mother?' Jock repeats slowly, as if trying to comprehend it himself. 'You kept that pretty secret.'

'It wasn't a secret. We just didn't advertise it.'

'You don't look alike,' I observe.

'I probably look like my dad, whoever the hell he is.'

'So your mum got pregnant with you—'

'When she was working, yes. It happens. Right, are you two going to stand around gawping all day, or are you going to get some clothes on and get to work?'

'What happens if we decide we don't want to work here any more?' Jock asks softly.

'Then you pack your bags and fuck off.'

'You owe us a week's pay.'

'You're having a laugh. You seriously expect to be paid when you've been swanning around enjoying free board and lodging at Madame's expense?' She marches over to one of the fridges. 'Where's all the food gone?'

'We had to give most of it away,' Jock explains. 'It would have gone off otherwise.'

She narrows her eyes as she stares at him, evidently trying to work out if he's pulled a fast one or not. 'Fine,' she says eventually. 'This is how it's going to go. I'm going to draw a line under last week but anything you eat and drink in here from now on comes out of your wages. Do you understand?'

'Perfectly,' Jock replies. 'We won't hold you up any longer, will we, Beatrice?' He gently takes my hand and starts to lead me out of the kitchen.

'Oi!' Maria cries. 'What about all of this?' She waves at the two plates and cups of cappuccino.

'Oh, I made that for you,' he tells her. 'Welcome home and bon appetit.'

Neither of us speaks until we're safely in the sanctuary of Jock's bedroom on the top floor.

'The sooner we go, the better,' I say to him. 'There's no way I'm working for her.'

'Agreed. Let's shower and pack, then get the hell out of here.'

10

There's no sign of Maria when we get back down to the kitchen, but the two congealed plates of bacon and eggs are still on the worktop, along with the cold cappuccinos. She hasn't even turned off the coffee machine, I notice. I'm tempted to leave everything as it is – after all, it's not my problem any more – but I know I can't. With a sigh, I switch off the coffee machine, scrape the food into the bin and pour the coffee away before washing everything up. Jock has grabbed his knife roll and is rootling in the drawers, pulling various objects out and piling them on the worktop.

'I'm not leaving anything behind that I bought,' he tells me when I raise my eyebrows. 'Madame may have liked everything just so, but she was as tight as a duck's arse when it came to buying equipment, so a lot of this stuff is mine.'

'*Comme le derrière d'un canard*,' I joke.

'Exactly. Can you give me a hand with this?'

We're just loading up a plastic bag with the equipment Jock is taking when Maria reappears.

'What the hell do you think you're doing?' she asks accusingly. 'You'd better not be nicking that stuff.'

'I'm only taking what's mine,' Jock tells her forcefully. 'And even if I was stealing it, what are you going to do? Call the police? Oh, and in case you haven't worked it out yet, I quit.'

'Me too,' I add.

'What? Why?' Despite being incredibly unpleasant from the moment she walked through the door, it obviously hasn't crossed her mind that we might follow through on our threat to leave.

'Oddly,' I tell her coolly, 'we have a problem with your business model.'

'What do you mean? It never bothered you before.'

'That's because we didn't know what was going on before. You can't seriously expect us to turn a blind eye while you carry on an illegal business that's exploiting vulnerable women.'

'Oh, I get it,' she sneers. 'You don't want to get your hands dirty now you know about our little sideline. But, before you come over all holier-than-thou, you sanctimonious little bitch, ask yourself this: where do you think all the girls we had working for us are now, eh? I'll tell you. They're probably on the streets servicing the fucking weirdos out there, and relying on pimps who will quickly get them hooked on drugs to control them. They'll have to do more and more tricks to fund the drugs, and they'll need more and more drugs to make doing the tricks bearable. If they're lucky, they'll get put up in some filthy, rat-infested squat, and they'll have to service punters there too, like a conveyor belt. They'll probably die of an overdose or choking on their own vomit. Of course, that's assuming they don't get murdered by a punter first. At least they were safe here. This place is a sanctuary in comparison.'

'Sanctuary?' Jock laughs humourlessly. 'That's not the word I'd use.'

'That's because you're just as bloody ignorant as her. I expect you grew up in a nice middle-class home with hot meals on the table three times a day. You've never been forced to sell yourself just to survive. If you had, you'd realise just what a good deal it was working here. Anyway, I can't be arsed to argue with you two fuckwits any more. If that's how you feel, you can leave at the end of your notice period. In the meantime, I need you to help me make the beds.'

'No. We're going now,' Jock tells her.

'I don't think so. You need to give notice. It's in your contract.'

'I don't remember you being so concerned about our contracts when you told us to "pack our bags and fuck off" earlier.'

Jock's landed a blow. I can tell because it takes her a while to decide what to say next.

'Fine,' she blusters eventually. 'Play it like that if you want. It's no skin off my nose; I can manage quite happily without you and your shitty attitudes. But don't think of asking for a reference, because there's no bloody way I'm giving either of you one.'

'That's just fine,' I reply sweetly. 'A reference from you is the last thing I want.'

I'm shaking as we drag our bags to the door. It's not that I'm particularly afraid of conflict; I wouldn't be a very good manager if I was. But there was something so malevolent about Maria that I actually wouldn't have been surprised if she'd physically attacked us when we turned our backs on her. The relief when I step out onto the street is short-lived, however, as an awkward silence descends between Jock and me.

'I guess this is it then,' he says eventually. 'Which station are you heading to?'

'Paddington. You?'

'Kings Cross.'

'Right. Well...' He peters out.

This is really uncomfortable. How is it that we could do all the things we've done together this week and suddenly not know what to say to each other? In the end, I step forward and wrap my arms around him. His arms come up and pull me close as I bury my head in his chest and breathe him in. Although we've been perfectly upfront with each other about our relationship being time limited, there's a big part of me that doesn't want to let him go.

'Thank you,' I murmur into his shirt. 'For everything.'

He gently loosens his grip, holding me by my shoulders at arms' length as we look into each other's eyes. 'Thank you,' he replies. 'Apart from the police thing, this has been one of the best weeks of my life.'

'Mine too,' I agree.

'Do you want to keep in touch?'

'Sure.'

He smiles as we swap numbers, and I'm glad to have given the right answer. I think, deep down, we both know it won't happen. As soon as we're both settled in new jobs, we'll be flat-out busy again and the time we spent together will become nothing but a distant memory. All we're doing is fooling ourselves, so parting doesn't feel so final.

'OK,' he says decisively. 'Kings Cross, here I come. Safe travels, Beatrice, and I'll see you around.'

'Safe travels yourself,' I reply, before giving him a quick final kiss. He turns and starts to walk towards the main road, and I stand and watch until he's out of sight.

* * *

I'm in a reflective mood as my taxi heads towards Paddington station. I'm thinking about Jock, obviously, but I'm also trying to decide whether I should call DI Winter and let her know what Maria is planning. It's the right thing to do, but she might want to interview me again, and I don't want to go anywhere near that custody suite. By the time the taxi drops me off, I've decided. That doesn't stop me feeling nervous as I pull out her card and dial the number, but I know I won't be able to sleep easily if I don't do it.

'DI Winter speaking,' she says when the call connects.

'Hello, this is Beatrice Fairhead. You interviewed me in connection with Eileen Strickland?'

'I remember you, Beatrice. What's up?'

'Can I give you some information in confidence, without coming in and being interviewed?'

'Of course. What is it?'

I tell her about Maria being Eileen's daughter, which she already knew. Their plan for Eileen to take the hit to allow Maria to stay free is obviously news, but when I tell her she's planning to reopen the brothel just as before, she laughs softly.

'What?' I ask.

'That's exactly what we suspected she was going to do. Thank you for the information, Beatrice. We'll be keeping a very close eye on her, don't worry.'

* * *

I'd forgotten how long the train from London to Ludlow takes. With a change at Crewe, the overall journey time is predicted to be over three hours. With nothing else to distract me, I fish out the digital camera and scroll through the photos I've taken during Jock's and my week together. We certainly crammed a lot in. There are selfies at most of the tourist attractions we visited, as well as a surprising number of photos of the various dishes Jock prepared in the evenings. There's a lovely one of him doing the flambé, which makes me smile. He's seriously talented; I don't think I've ever eaten so well. Someone will snap him up, no doubt.

To begin with, the scenery outside the window is the urban landscape I'm used to. London is not at its prettiest from the railway – too much concrete and graffiti – but I feel affection for it nonetheless. Shropshire is beautiful but very rural, so London always seemed like a glittering world full of amazing possibilities when I was growing up. As we leave the city behind and the view changes to fields and trees, my mood only darkens.

This is temporary, I remind myself. *I'll be back before I know it.* It doesn't seem to help.

By the time the train finally rattles into Ludlow station, it seems the weather has come out in sympathy with me, as the sky has darkened and heavy rain has started to fall. There's no canopy over the platform, so the few of us that disembark are decidedly bedraggled by the time we've crossed the bridge over the tracks to reach the ticket hall. My mood isn't improved when I realise that there's no sign of my dad, despite me texting him earlier with my arrival time. I pull out my phone to see if I've missed a message, but there's nothing. I flick through the list of numbers until I find his mobile.

'Hi, Beatrice,' he answers when the call connects. 'I haven't forgotten you, I'm just a bit held up. I don't suppose there are any taxis at the station, are there?'

I look out of the window at the bare taxi rank. 'No, Dad,' I tell him. 'There never are.'

'OK,' he sighs. 'Give me half an hour to sort this and I'll be with you.'

At least there are a couple of seats in the ticket office, so I plonk myself down on one of them to wait. After around ten minutes, I'm surprised to see a taxi splash to a halt in the rank outside. Grabbing my case, I hurry out. The driver lowers his window a fraction.

'Are you Clare?' he asks.

'No, Beatrice. Why?'

'I'm here for Clare.'

'Oh, right.'

'Did you need a taxi then?'

'Yes please.'

'Sorry, love. If you didn't pre-book, you've got no chance. Everyone will be flat out in this weather. Next time you come, it would be a good idea to book in advance.'

'Right. Thanks.'

Our unhelpful conversation is cut short by the arrival of a substantial woman in her mid-forties. As soon as she confirms her name to the driver, he transforms into a model of courtesy, jumping out of the car to help her put her bag in the boot.

'Are you all right there?' she says to me as the driver opens the door for her.

'Yes, fine. I was looking for a taxi, but this gentleman has just explained that I ought to have pre-booked.'

'Where are you going? Maybe we can share.'

'The Bideford Arms hotel.'

Her face cracks open into a wide smile. 'What a coincidence! That's exactly where I'm going. Hop in and we'll go together. I'm Clare, by the way.'

'Beatrice. Are you sure you don't mind?'

'Not at all.'

The driver looks decidedly less than impressed by this turn of events, but helps me put my case in the boot nonetheless.

'This is very kind of you,' I say to her as the taxi pulls away. 'Let me get the fare, at least.'

'Absolutely not,' she says firmly. 'I'm putting it on expenses, so don't worry.'

'Are you here on business then?' I ask.

'Yes, you?'

'Leisure. My parents own the Bideford Arms, and I'm staying with them for a bit.'

'How lovely. I expect they'll be delighted to see you. I hope you don't mind me saying, but you look familiar. Have we met before?'

'I don't think so. I've probably just got one of those faces.'

'Yes, maybe that's it.'

The hotel is just as I remember it when we pull up. Clare pays the driver and we grab our bags from the boot.

'Aren't you coming?' she asks when I don't immediately follow her towards the front door.

'No. I get to use the tradesmen's entrance round the back,' I tell her.

'Nonsense. You'll get soaked. I'm sure your parents won't mind. Come on.'

I follow her reluctantly into the reception area. The faint smell of polish and sandalwood air freshener takes me straight back to my childhood, as does the floral-patterned carpet and the textured wallpaper.

'Thank you again for the lift,' I say to Clare as my mother appears behind the counter. 'I hope you enjoy your stay.'

'You too,' she replies. 'It was lovely to meet you. I just wish I could work out why you look so familiar.'

I'm very aware of my mother's disapproving stare as I manoeuvre my case through the door marked *Private* next to the reception desk that leads to the annexe where my parents live. To my surprise, my father is sitting at the kitchen table, sipping a cup of tea.

'Oh, hello, love,' he says when he spots me. 'I was just about to come and get you. There was a spot of bother with the sink in room twelve, but I've sorted it and I was just having a quick swig before setting off.'

'Looks like I've saved you the trouble then,' I tell him, trying hard not to feel hurt that he evidently thinks a cup of tea is more important than collecting his only child from the station like he'd agreed.

'The kettle's not long boiled if you want a cup. You know where everything is.'

As if to emphasise how unremarkable my arrival is, he turns his attention to the newspaper that's lying open on the kitchen table, turning the pages until he finds the crossword and grabbing a pencil from the pot on the windowsill behind him. Flicking the kettle back on, I pull a mug out of the cupboard, add a teabag and I'm just about to retrieve the milk from the fridge when my mother bustles in.

'Beatrice, what were you *thinking*?' she exclaims.

'Sorry?'

'Not only did you use the guest entrance, but Mrs Evans informed me that you also shared a taxi from the station. Do you have any idea how inappropriate it is to accept hospitality from our guests? Especially as she nearly recognised you. I thought we agreed you were going to keep a low profile.'

'I tried, but what was I supposed to do? If it wasn't for her, I'd probably still be at the station.' I glance angrily at Dad, but he's oblivious, his nose firmly in the crossword.

'You might as well have stuck a banner on the hotel announcing your arrival,' Mum scolds. 'Heaven help us if that woman puts two and two together. Please tell me you paid your half of the fare, at least.'

'No. She offered. She said she could claim it on expenses.'

'It's still not right.'

'Nice to see you too, Mum,' I mutter sarcastically.

'Don't be like that. Of course we're pleased to see you, darling. It's just that the manner of your arrival was rather *unorthodox*, and it threw me. How are you? You look like you've put on weight.'

I sigh. I wasn't expecting the red-carpet treatment, but this is a new low, even for them. The shorter my stay here, the better.

11

———

I was first put to work in the hotel the day after my thirteenth birthday. Mum and Dad had researched it carefully to make sure they weren't falling foul of any laws and, to be fair, I didn't mind. I started as a pot washer, but I graduated to preparing the rooms for the arrival of guests over the summer holidays. I loved it, and I took a great deal of pride in my work. They also paid me fairly and monitored my hours to make sure that I wasn't working more than I should be. As I grew, they gave me more responsibility and I was a regular behind the check-in desk by the time I went away to university. It's therefore no surprise that I'm expected to pitch in now that I'm back; in fact, I'm delighted to have something to do. What is a surprise is that Mum is studiously avoiding giving me anything that might bring me into contact with actual guests.

'It's for your own good,' she told me firmly when I asked about it. 'I'd hate for a guest to recognise you and say something nasty. We got away with it once; best not to tempt fate.'

What this means is that I'm back at the bottom of the heap, cleaning rooms and preparing them for guests, sorting out laundry and stuff like that. Although I don't mind the work, it does mean that I have quite a lot of downtime in the evenings. Normally, I'd be helping to serve dinner, but that's obviously forbidden, so I've largely spent them in my room, sending my CV to various agencies, transferring the pictures from the camera to my phone, scrolling through them and fighting the temptation to message Jock. I did get in touch with a couple of my old school friends who still live locally and we talked about organising a night out, but Mum practically hit the ceiling when I mentioned it to her. I may be an adult, but I'm well and truly grounded while I'm here. Mum's made it perfectly clear that one of the conditions of me staying is that I remain completely out of sight.

I'm sitting at the kitchen table with Dad when my phone rings on Thursday afternoon. The caller ID tells me it's one of the agencies I've registered with and I nearly drop it in my haste to answer.

'Beatrice Fairhead,' I say in my most professional voice. Dad raises his eyebrows, obviously curious, so I slip out of the kitchen and head for my room.

'Beatrice, it's Alice from Baxter Associates. Is now a good time?'

'Yes, absolutely.'

'Great. I've put your CV in front of a number of potential employers, but it seems that finding you a position is proving rather more difficult than I predicted when we spoke at the beginning of the week.'

This is not the news I was hoping for, and my spirits instantly plummet again.

'Oh? How come?' I ask. She told me there were loads of vacancies on Tuesday, so I'll be quite annoyed if it turns out she was leading me on.

'Your CV is impressive, there's no doubt about that, but everyone I've sent it to is understandably nervous about employing someone with an association to Hotel Dufour. It's a small world, Beatrice, and they all know about what was going on there.'

'But you explained to them that I wasn't a part of it, didn't you?'

'Of course I did, but they're risk-averse. You know as well as I do that reputation counts for everything in this industry. However, the good news is that I do have an idea, if you're prepared to think outside the box a little.'

'I'm listening.'

'I rang a friend of mine at an agency that specialises in providing hospitality on film sets, and she's got something she thinks might be perfect for you.'

* * *

Mum has joined Dad in the kitchen when I walk back in a little while later. They're trying to act nonchalant but it's obvious that they're desperate to find out who was on the phone.

'I've got an interview,' I tell them.

'Of course you have, darling,' Mum gushes. 'You're so pretty and charming and clever. Is it one of the big London hotels?'

'The Dorchester,' Dad interrupts. 'No, the Savoy. Although, having said that, I could see you at Claridge's. I watched the TV series about that; it's right up your street.'

'It's not a hotel. It's a film set, actually.'

'A *film set*?' Mum looks horrified. 'What would a film set want with someone like you? You don't know anything about films.'

'I don't know yet,' I reply testily. 'I've got a call with someone called Sandra from an agency that deals with this kind of thing, so I expect she'll tell me more. Alice wouldn't have put me forward if she didn't think I was suitable, would she?'

'I don't trust these agents,' Mum counters. 'Only out for what they can get, that's what they are. What does it matter to them if the job is suitable, as long as they pocket their commission. You should tell this woman you're not interested. Stick to what you know.'

'The problem is that nobody in the hotel industry will touch me at the moment. They all know about Hotel Dufour and don't want to be tainted by association.'

'That's ridiculous,' Mum scoffs.

'Is it?' I accuse. 'You're doing just the same thing, keeping me as far away from the guests as possible because you don't want your precious reputation to be dented.'

'We're just looking out for you! You know how cruel people can be, and that woman you arrived with nearly recognised you.'

Thankfully, my phone rings again before this conversation can go any further.

'Beatrice, this is Sandra from The Appleford Agency. Is now a good time?'

'Absolutely,' I tell her as I slip out of the kitchen once more.

'So, I've received your CV and Alice has explained your, erm, predicament. As it happens, I do have a vacancy that might suit you, but I need to ask you a couple of questions before I put your name forward. The position I'm thinking about is a two-month contract. Is that likely to be an issue?'

'I was hoping for something permanent,' I tell her, trying to hide my disappointment.

'Pretty much all the positions we deal with are fixed-term contracts,' she explains. 'Film work is very project based but, if you do well, there's no reason why we wouldn't be able to put you forward for other contracts when this one finishes. And each one will push Hotel Dufour further from the top of your CV, think of it that way.'

'Can you tell me more about the position?'

'Absolutely. The company is called Casterbridge Media, and they're looking for someone to take care of the contestants in a new reality show they're shooting in Mallorca. It says on your CV that you're fluent in Spanish. I don't mean to sound sceptical, but some people are prone to exaggeration on their CVs, and this is a key skill for the role.'

'It's not exaggerated. I am fluent.'

'Good. The contestants and crew will all be English, but you'll need to act as interpreter where needed.'

'That won't be a problem.'

'Good. I'll send them your CV and let you know.'

'Thank you, Sandra.'

* * *

Having had time to come to terms with the concept, Mum and Dad are now almost more excited than me about the potential job. I'd like to hope that this is because they're genuinely pleased for me, but I suspect it's mainly because it means I'll move out again. I did explain that it was only for two months, but I think they've chosen not to hear that bit. Nevertheless, it's fair to say that we were all delighted when Sandra called back the next day to say that the production company wanted to set up an online interview at eleven o'clock on Monday morning.

By half past ten, I'm as ready as I can be. I've put my hair up, dressed in the suit Mum warily allowed me to go out and buy, and applied just enough make-up to give the impression (I hope) that I care about my appearance without being vain. I connect to the meeting using the link Sandra has sent and wait anxiously for my interviewer to join. When he does, five minutes after the meeting was supposed to have begun, I'm a little surprised to be confronted by a man who doesn't look a day older than me. I don't know why, but I expected someone closer to my parents' age.

'Hello, Beatrice,' he says, smiling widely to reveal suspiciously even teeth. 'I'm so sorry I'm late. My previous call overran. I'm Gus, by the way, and I'm one of the producers at Casterbridge Media.'

'Nice to meet you, Gus,' I reply.

'Tell me what you know about the role.'

'Not a huge amount, I'm afraid. I know it's a reality TV show and that it's set in Mallorca. That's all they told me.'

'Let me fill in the blanks for you then. The show is called *Too Busy for Love*, and the premise is that we take a load of people whose lives are so jam-packed that they don't have time for dating, put them in a sumptuous villa for six weeks and try to pair them up. Think of a cross between *First Dates Hotel* and *Love Island*.'

'Sounds interesting,' I tell him. 'What would you need from me?'

'So, we have local people to cook, clean the house and so on, but your role would be best described as guest liaison cum supervisor. You'd be responsible for making sure dietary and other requirements are fully catered for, dealing with the local contractors and generally ensuring that the house runs smoothly. Sandra tells me your background is hospitality?'

He's either not read my CV or he has no idea about Hotel Dufour, I realise.

'That's right,' I tell him. 'My most recent role was managing a hotel in London, so I'm well versed in all the duties you've mentioned. Hopefully, Sandra also mentioned that I'm fluent in Spanish?'

'She did, which was a big plus point. Do you mind me asking why you left your previous position?'

'I'm looking for a new challenge,' I say, pleased with my deflection. I haven't lied, I've just not told him everything.

'And you have a driving licence?'

'Yes.' Again, not a lie, even if I haven't driven in years. I may hardly know Gus, but he seems nice, and I'm actually quite keen to get this job, even though it's out of my comfort zone.

'Great. If we offer you the post, you'll be the first person travelling out, so we'll arrange for a hire car to be waiting for you at the airport. The crew will follow a couple of days after you, and then the cast at the end. We've rented accommodation nearby for the crew, but you'll need to stay in the main house with the cast in case they need you in the middle of the night. You'll be on call 24/7.'

'That's fine; I'm used to that. Are you able to give me any indication of the start date?'

'It's soon. I don't know if Sandra told you that we had someone lined up for this role, but he dropped us in it at the last minute. Better offer, apparently. We'd need you to fly out on Thursday. Is that a problem?'

'Not at all.'

The rest of the interview runs pretty smoothly. Gus doesn't throw me any curve-ball questions, and he seems to be pretty happy with the answers I'm giving him. As well as the duties already described, one of my roles will be to control the housekeeping cost, so we talk about that for a while. Basically, while the budget is fairly generous, the guests won't be eating caviar and drinking champagne all day every day. The salary is a little less than I was getting at Hotel Dufour, but there are fewer people to look after so I'm not really surprised. It all seems eminently doable and, after an hour or so, Gus starts to wrap up.

'Look,' he tells me. 'I think you're a good fit and we don't have any other candidates, so I'm not going to mess you about. The job's yours if you want it. Do you?'

'Yes, absolutely.'

'Great. I'll get Sandra to organise the paperwork, and we'll be in touch with all the details later today. I look forward to meeting you in person. Oh, and you'll also get an email from my colleague Dom, which will give you the list of everything we need you to do before we get there. Have you got any questions before we wrap up?'

'I don't think so at the moment, but would it be a good idea if I took your phone number just in case anything unexpected comes up?'

'Such as?' He looks suddenly rattled. 'You're not going to drop out on us as well, are you?'

'No!' I tell him emphatically. 'But if I get there and there's a problem with the house or something, I expect you'd want to know, wouldn't you?'

'If you get there and there's a problem with the house, I expect you to fix it,' he says with a smile. 'However, I will make sure the email Dom sends has our contact details on it in case of emergencies. Anything else?'

'No.'

'Fabulous. See you in Mallorca!'

* * *

Mum and Dad are both waiting expectantly in the kitchen.

'How did you get on?' Mum asks.

'Good. I got the job. I fly to Mallorca on Thursday.'

'So soon?' Dad is trying to look like he's upset but doing a spectacularly poor job of it.

'They had another candidate, but he dropped out, apparently.'

'You aren't going to be on camera, are you?' Mum asks warily.

'I wouldn't have thought so. Why?'

'It's just... well, you know.'

'I'm not sure I do.'

'Your *history*,' she says theatrically. 'What if someone recognises you and calls the TV company?'

I've had enough. 'Mum. You really need to get over this. I'm not Britney Spears shaving her head; I'm a complete nobody who did nothing wrong and I'm sure everyone has forgotten about me. Even if I do appear on camera, nobody is going to recognise me or care.'

'You can't know that. I just have your best interests at heart. Perhaps you should call them and make sure you won't appear.'

'For God's sake!' I shout. 'I'm not a criminal. Stop treating me like one.'

There's a deathly silence for a few seconds, before my mother bursts into tears and rushes from the room. Dad pushes back his chair wearily and starts to follow her.

'I know you and your mother don't always see eye to eye,' he tells me heavily, 'but she does love you, and sometimes I think you forget that.'

I can feel furious tears pricking my own eyes, but I know Dad will always side with Mum over me, so there's no point in trying to tell him how she makes me feel. Instead, I turn and flee back to my bedroom.

Thursday cannot come soon enough.

12

_____

As I step out of the terminal building into the Mallorcan sunshine, it's like a heavy weight has been lifted from my shoulders. Although Dad did manage to broker a truce between Mum and me, it wasn't an easy one. I did get a little more freedom and actually managed to meet a couple of my school friends for a drink last night, but I've paid for it in expressive sighs and barbed comments. Losing my rag with her was an idiotic thing for me to do, I know. For as long as I can remember, our family has revolved around keeping Mum happy, because the consequences of doing otherwise were always so catastrophic. She doesn't sulk, exactly, but she holds on to the hurt like a trophy for weeks. It wouldn't surprise me if she's still nursing a grudge when I get back from this trip.

It was lovely to catch up with Louise and Rachel, though. I haven't seen them in ages but it was like we just picked up where we'd left off years ago. We were in the pub till closing time, and they seemed particularly interested in my week with Jock.

'What I don't get,' Rachel had argued at one point, 'is how you can spend a week with someone who is so patently right for you, and then just walk away at the end of it. What if he's the one?'

'I don't think you can tell if someone is the one after a week,' I'd countered. 'He is lovely, and maybe we'd have made a go of it if things had been different, but he's gone back to Scotland and I'm off to Mallorca. We both need jobs, and long-distance relationships don't work.'

'I guess you're right. Anyway, if the universe wants you together, I'm sure it'll find a way to make it happen.'

Louise and I had both laughed at this; Rachel is a great believer in the power of the universe and our ability to manifest things into being if we want them enough, so it was only going to be a matter of time before she brought it into the conversation.

The evening was such a success that even Mum's scowl when I finally got home last night didn't dent my good mood. Dad did offer to drive me to the airport but I opted to take the train, even though it takes nearly twice as long. He tried to sound disappointed, but the relief shone out of him like a beacon. I'm sure they're just as delighted as I am that I've gone. I plan to use any downtime while I'm out here to try to line something up for when I get back; I'm prepared to do almost anything to avoid going back home.

The queue at the car-hire desk is relatively short, but it still takes nearly an hour before I'm finally handed the keys and told where to find my car. When I get there, my mouth drops open in horror. I had visions of a nippy little runabout, but this is a minibus. Thinking there must be some mistake, I rejoin the queue but, when I finally reach the desk again, the agent informs me in rapid Spanish that the TV company was adamant I should have the largest vehicle available. His attitude makes it very clear he's not open to negotiation so, in frustration, I call Gus.

'Please tell me you're in Mallorca,' are his opening words when the call connects.

'Of course I am,' I tell him.

'Good. What's up?'

'Why have you hired me this enormous bus? I've never driven anything as big as this before.'

'It's just like any other car, isn't it? I'm sure you'll get used to the size quickly enough. I've hired the same for me, but Dom doesn't drive and we can't all get in one car, so we'll need you to meet us when we land on Sunday. You'll also be doing airport runs for some of the cast, so learn the route, OK? See you in a few days.'

Great. Not only have I been stitched up with a ridiculous car that was never mentioned at the interview, but I'm also expected to be an airport shuttle driver. With a growl of frustration, I press the button on the key fob to unlock it, shove my bag in the cavernous boot and climb into the driving seat. Things only go from bad to worse as I survey the controls. Not only is this thing massive, but the lack of clutch pedal indicates that it's also automatic, and I've never driven an automatic before. This is not a conversation for Gus, so I bite the bullet and ring my dad.

'Hello, darling, what's up?' he asks when he picks up.

'I'm in Mallorca and the hire car they've arranged for me is automatic. How do I drive one of those?'

'It's easy. Can you see the gear selector? It's normally on the floor where you'd find a normal gear lever.'

'No.'

'OK. Sometimes they're on the steering column or sticking out of the dash.'

Fifteen minutes later, we've found the selector on the steering column and he's talked me through everything he thinks I need to know. There was a brief panic when I couldn't find the handbrake, but we discovered that's automatic too, and I've shunted the bus in and out of the car parking space a couple of times just to make sure I understand what's going on. I've discovered that it has a camera and sensors on the back, so hopefully I'll manage not to run anybody over while reversing at least. I've put the address of the villa into the satnav, so the only thing left to do is pluck up the courage and go. I'm still deeply anxious about taking this thing out on the road though, and my hands are sweating as I fasten my seatbelt and ease out of the car parking space heading for the exit.

My next problem makes itself apparent immediately. I'm used to sitting on the right when I drive, and it's difficult enough to judge the width of this thing without trying to do it from the wrong seat. I very nearly take out the gatepost at the exit, and my heart is thumping as I join the highway towards Palma. Thankfully, this road is a wide dual carriageway so I've got plenty of space around me. There are a couple of hairy moments when the traffic grinds to a halt and I accidentally hit the brake with both feet because I'm automatically reaching for the clutch, but I'm starting to feel a little less intimidated by the size of the car by the time I reach my turn-off. Unfortunately, the roads then start getting progressively smaller and narrower until, after a particularly fractious episode when I meet a tractor coming the other way and have to reverse for what feels like miles, I'm cursing Gus and Casterbridge Media with a vengeance. When I finally pull up at the gates of Villa Madrigal, I'm a sweaty mess and I reckon the stress has shortened my life by at least a year.

'*Hola, ¿cómo puedo ayudarte?*' a disembodied female voice says after I press the buzzer by the gate.

'*Hola, soy Beatrice de Casterbridge Media. Creo que estás esperándome,*' I reply.

'*Sí, sí, pasa*,' the voice cries enthusiastically as the huge gates silently start to swing open.

Once inside the gates, I find myself on a gravelled track which seems to go on for ever. I must have been driving for at least five minutes past paddocks containing sleek-looking horses, stables and cottages before the main house finally comes into view. I remember Gus mentioning that it was sumptuous, but this is something else. The driveway widens into a sweeping circle in front of the house, with a fountain in the middle of it. When I pictured the villa in my mind, I envisaged something like you see when you search online, but this is enormous. The rough stone walls and red tiled roof help it to blend into its landscape, as if it's been here forever. It must be hundreds of years old.

I'm barely out of the car before a diminutive woman comes hurrying out of the house to greet me. She must be under five feet tall and looks like she's somewhere in her mid-fifties.

'*¡Madre de Dios!*' she exclaims when she catches sight of the minibus. 'Why is it so big?'

'The TV company insisted,' I tell her in matching Spanish. 'I'm Beatrice.'

'Rosa. Your Spanish is excellent!'

'Thank you.' Although I told Sandra and Gus that I was fluent, it's a while since I've actually spoken Spanish, so I'm relieved that it's come back so easily. 'My mother is Spanish, so she made sure I grew up able to speak the language. Is this your house, Rosa?'

She laughs. 'Goodness, no. It belongs to an Italian businessman called Salvatore Mancini. He comes each year with his family for a month early in the summer, before it gets too hot, and lets it out the rest of the time. My husband, Pedro, and I look after the house for him, welcome guests and so on. Come inside, let me show you around.'

Although the sun is high in the sky and the temperature outside must be nearly thirty degrees, it's deliciously cool in the house, courtesy of the thick stone walls, I'm sure. It's also surprisingly dark.

'We close the shutters during the day to keep the heat out,' Rosa explains as she flicks on the lights. We're standing in a double-height hallway, with a gorgeous open-beamed ceiling above us. There are doors on both sides and a magnificent curved staircase at the far end with another large doorway underneath it that I guess leads out into the gardens.

'The place was pretty much a ruin when Mr Mancini bought it,' Rosa tells me as she leads me through one of the doors into an enormous sitting room with sofas and chairs arranged around tables. There must be seating for nearly thirty people in here. 'The roof had fallen in and everything was rotten. But he loved the location and saw the potential. It took five years to get the house restored. Everything had to be correct. Mr Mancini is a stickler for detail.'

'It's gorgeous,' I observe.

'It is. He has done a beautiful job. Come and see the dining room.'

She leads me through to another huge room with a long table down the middle.

'We can seat twenty in here comfortably, or twenty-six at a push,' she informs me. 'However, most of our guests prefer to eat outside. I'll show you in a minute.'

The next room is the kitchen, which is beautifully appointed but surprisingly compact compared to the grandeur of the other rooms I've seen. Rosa smiles as she sees my confusion. 'You are thinking that this room is too small to be able to prepare food for so many guests, yes?'

'I am,' I agree.

'This is what we call the family kitchen,' she explains. 'Guests can come in here to make themselves a snack if they wish. We keep the fridges fully stocked with fresh fruit, water, and whatever other alcoholic and non-alcoholic drinks they request, so they can help themselves whenever they want. The main kitchen is through here.' She leads me through another door, where I'm confronted by the kind of kitchen that I imagine would get Jock salivating. It's a sea of pristine stainless steel with a full-sized pass.

'Wow,' I breathe.

'This is my kitchen,' Rosa states proudly, stroking the pass. 'Before we moved here, Pedro and I had our own restaurant in Palma. Mr Mancini used to visit every time he came to check up on the house and, how can I put it, he made us an offer we couldn't refuse. I loved the restaurant, but it's a hard business to be in. So when Mr Mancini told me I could design the kitchen just as I wanted it, plus we could have accommodation in one of the cottages and a generous salary guaranteed, it wasn't an easy decision, but we both knew it was the right one.'

'What does Pedro do?' I ask.

'He's the main caretaker of the house and gardens. He's very clever with his hands; there's almost nothing he can't fix, and I think he's the only person in the world who truly understands the filtration system for the swimming pool. He's gone into Palma to get some things, but you'll meet him when he returns. There's lots more to see; follow me.'

By the time the tour is complete, nearly an hour later, I can completely see why Casterbridge Media chose this house. The rest of the ground floor is made up of a games room with a full-sized snooker table, a home cinema room, a TV room, a study and a library, all beautifully appointed. Upstairs, the twelve large bedrooms all have king-sized beds and ensuite bathrooms. Rosa

watches me with amusement as I flick automatically into professional mode, checking under the duvets and pillowcases to make
sure everything is spotlessly clean and perfectly pressed,
ensuring that the bottles of shampoo, shower gel and conditioner
in the bathrooms are properly filled and that there is at least one
spare toilet roll. Everything passes muster, including the beautifully fluffy towels and bath robes.

'I can see you've done this before,' Rosa remarks as we make
our way back downstairs.

'I come from the hotel business,' I tell her. 'Sorry, I hope you
weren't offended.'

'Not at all. It shows that you're a professional. I just wish I'd
known this about you before you came.'

'Why?'

'I would have hidden something to see if you found it,' she
tells me with a mischievous glint in her eyes. 'Before I show you
where you will be sleeping, let me take you outside.'

She leads me out of the door underneath the staircase onto a
wide terrace that spans the entire rear of the house. A long table
sits underneath a canopy on the terrace, which has stairs at each
end leading down to the gardens and the pool. The gardens are
beautiful; verdant lawns fill the gaps between flowerbeds that are
riots of colour. Healthy-looking trees provide welcome patches of
shade. It's a stark contrast to the arid landscape I drove through
to get here.

'Villa Madrigal has its own underground spring,' Rosa tells
me, once more reading my thoughts. 'Water is not an issue for us,
and Mr Mancini is very proud of the garden.'

'Who looks after it?'

'Pedro, but the watering system is all automated. You'll see
when it comes on this evening. Would you like to look at the
pool?'

'Yes.'

The pool area is laid out with luxurious-looking sunbeds, umbrellas for shade, and a bar.

'We stock that like the family kitchen, so guests can help themselves,' Rosa explains as I examine the bar. 'Obviously, it's up to you, but we don't normally put alcoholic drinks down here. Alcohol and swimming pools are not generally a good mixture.'

'I agree. Soft drinks only down here unless the production company has firm views to the contrary.'

The pool itself is large and looks very inviting. I slip off my shoe and dip my toe in the water. Unsurprisingly, the temperature is perfect. Cool enough to be refreshing without being shockingly cold.

'I hope you will have time for a swim before the rest of the guests arrive,' Rosa suggests. 'You need to check everything, I think.'

'I'll make time,' I assure her.

She leads me back into the house, through the main kitchen to a door I hadn't noticed before, marked *Privado*.

'This is your accommodation,' she says, opening the door and handing me the key. 'It's far enough away from the guests that they won't disturb you if they stay up late, but close enough that you can get to them quickly if they need you.'

Although it's nowhere near as lavish as the rest of the house, I'm not disappointed. There's a small sitting room with a sofa and a TV, a basic kitchen, a decent-sized bedroom with a large wardrobe, and a surprisingly well-appointed bathroom with separate bath and shower. I even have my own door, which leads out to a large car parking space.

'What do you think?' Rosa asks.

I smile at her. I think I've landed in paradise.

13

I'm in good spirits as I leave Villa Madrigal to head for the airport on Sunday afternoon. The minibus still bothers me a little on the small roads, but Pedro has been helping me to practise with it. He and Rosa have enlisted me as their chauffeur for every errand they've had to run and, between them, that has amounted to quite a few. I've had to negotiate my way through narrow streets in the nearby villages, park it in seemingly impossible spots and reverse it for long distances when we've met things coming the other way on the tiny lanes. Pedro is the total opposite of Rosa; where she is small, chatty and inclined to screech 'watch out' at the top of her lungs every time she thinks I'm getting too close to something, he's a beanpole of a man with very few words. Needless to say, I find being with him in the car much more relaxing than driving her. They're patently devoted to each other, although she admitted to me that they did go through a rough patch not long after they were married when they discovered they were unable to have children. This might partly explain the way they seem to have semi-adopted me. Despite the fact that we've all been busy preparing for the arrival of the film crew and first set of guests, I haven't had to prepare a single meal for myself, as Rosa has insisted I eat breakfast, lunch and dinner with them each day.

I might be out of my comfort zone, but I've really enjoyed getting my teeth into this project. We've completed all the items on Gus's checklist, which helpfully included notes on the various dietary needs of the crew and the initial set of guests so Rosa and I could plan menus. The format of the show is fairly simple, if brutal. We start with ten guests, five men and five women. After that, new guests will arrive in pairs at regular intervals and, this is the brutal bit, choose whose places they are going to take after spending twenty-four hours with the group. The two people who are replaced are then sent home. I couldn't understand how someone who is purportedly too busy for love could commit to spending up to six weeks lounging around at Villa Madrigal, but my question was answered not only by the £50,000 prize money for the viewers' favourite couple at the end, but also when Pedro and I were dispatched to an office supplies shop in Palma to collect twelve flatpack desks, which he then erected in the bedrooms. On top of that, a truck arrived yesterday filled to the brim with boxes and cables which the driver informed us was filming equipment, much to Rosa's horror. We've stacked it all in the dining room, and I've noticed her eyeing it suspiciously every time she goes in there.

The latest missive from Dom had the daily schedule on it. Breakfast is to be served at seven each morning, and the contestants will have to remain downstairs until at least nine, while Rosa and I rush round cleaning their rooms. They are then allowed to work until lunchtime, and they have to be downstairs again by six thirty for pre-dinner drinks. Meals will be served buffet-style and eaten at the table outside unless the weather turns against us. The only exception is dinner, where two pairs will be chosen to have one-on-one meals away from the main group; I'm not sure how that is supposed to work yet, but I expect it will become clear soon enough.

The traffic is light and it doesn't take me long to reach the airport, where I score a further win by managing to secure one of the spots in the express parking lot directly outside the terminal. Although Pedro has assured me the minibus is just under the height restriction for the multi-storey, I don't fancy taking my chances in there. My mood improves even more when I reach the arrivals hall and see that the flight I'm meeting has already landed. Sure enough, Gus appears a short time later with four other people, all pushing heavily laden trolleys.

'Beatrice!' he exclaims, a smile breaking out on his face when he reaches me. 'Lovely to meet you in person at last. How is everything?'

'All good so far,' I reply as I shake his hand.

'Great. Let me introduce you to the others. This is Dom, who you've met via email.'

'Nice to meet you, Beatrice,' a tall, bearded man says.

'Dom is the associate producer and will be working closely with me,' Gus explains. 'Then we've got Chris and Tim here, who are our technical experts and camera operators. Finally' – he indicates an ebony-skinned woman with close-cropped hair – 'this is Raquel, our sex and relationships expert.'

'Lovely to meet you all,' I tell them. 'The car is just outside for those who are coming with me.'

'You'll be taking Chris and Tim,' Gus informs me. 'Dom, Raquel and I have a conference call with HQ shortly, so it makes sense for us to travel together.'

'Fine with me,' I tell him. Chris and Tim follow me out to the minibus while the others wander off in search of the car-hire desk.

'Did the truck arrive?' Chris asks as we start loading their cases into the boot.

'Yes. I've never seen so much stuff,' I reply as we put the seats down and start loading their cases into the back.

When we get back, I leave Chris and Tim going through the piles of equipment in the dining room, change into my bikini and wander down to the pool for a swim. It's going to be off-limits as soon as the contestants arrive, so I'm determined to make the most of it before then. When the heat starts to go out of the day, I come back up to the house for a shower before going to help Rosa in the main kitchen. I say 'help', but really I'm just standing by the pass chatting to her in Spanish while she prepares the dinner.

'I'm not at all happy about all those cables,' she complains for the umpteenth time. 'I won't let them make a mess in Mr Mancini's beautiful home. You tell them that, Beatrice.'

'I did,' I reassure her. 'They've promised me that they know just how to lay them so they're practically invisible, and they will leave the house just as they found it.'

'Hmph.' She shrugs her shoulders, clearly unconvinced. 'Where are the others? Dinner is nearly ready.'

I glance at my watch; nearly two hours have passed since I got back. Even with the car-hire queues, it shouldn't be taking this long. I'm just about to call Gus to find out what's going on when the buzzer sounds to indicate that someone is at the gates.

'I'll start plating up,' Rosa tells me. 'You go and greet them.'

'Everything OK?' I ask as I walk out to meet Gus, Dom and Raquel, who are climbing down from an identical minibus to mine. 'We were starting to worry.'

'We, umm, had a spot of difficulty,' Gus admits sheepishly. 'The car was a bit bigger than I thought it would be and, well, I've not driven anything quite this size before.'

'He misjudged the width when we met a tractor coming the other way,' Dom adds. 'Had a bit of an argument with a wall.'

Curiosity gets the better of me and I walk round to the other side of the minibus, which is now sporting some impressive gouges and scratches.

'Ah,' I say, unable to suppress a grin. 'Don't worry. It's insured, so they'll just give you another one if you take it back, and you'll soon get used to the size, I'm sure.'

If Gus realises I'm parroting his own condescending remarks back to him, he has the good grace to allow me my victory and says nothing.

'Rosa's just dishing up,' I explain as I lead them through the house. 'We thought we'd eat on the terrace to make the most of it before the guests arrive.'

'How are you getting on with her?' Gus asks quietly as we step through the back door. 'I found her a little prickly when I came to do the reconnaissance visit. I don't know whether it's just the language barrier or something else.'

'She's really nice, but she's very houseproud and understand-ably worried about how much mess you're going to make with all the filming equipment,' I tell him honestly. 'She practically had kittens when she saw how much there was on the lorry yesterday.'

He stiffens. 'It's not really any of her business. Our agreement is with Mr Mancini, not her, and we made it very clear in the paperwork what equipment we'd need to rig up. I'll be relying on you to keep her docile, OK?'

'I'll do my best, but she's not going to react well if you start smashing the place up.'

'We're not going to smash anything up. We're going to rig up a few cameras and lay a few cables, that's all. How come the table is laid for eight? There are only six of us.'

'I've invited Rosa and Pedro to join us. They've been incredibly hospitable to me since I've arrived, and they're just as much part of the crew as the rest of us.'

Gus just grunts and takes his place, turning to talk to Dom in a low murmur. Thankfully, the slight tension in the air is dispelled completely as we tuck into the generously filled bowls of gazpacho that Rosa and I bring out to start with. By the time we've finished the main course of *pollo al ajillo*, juicy pieces of chicken heavily fragranced with rosemary, garlic and white wine, the atmosphere is positively convivial. The wine is flowing and I'm relieved to see both Gus and Rosa are looking a lot more relaxed.

'What's your job on the show?' I ask Raquel, who's sitting next to me.

'I interviewed all the contestants as part of the selection process,' she tells me. 'So I know what kinds of things they're looking for in a partner, and I also know what qualities they bring to the table. Let's just say there are certain people who pair up very well together on paper, so I'm here to give them the appropriate nudges if they need them. I'm also going to be running some workshops on successful relationships, to give them the best chance of taking any budding romances back to the real world. Are you in a relationship?'

An image of Jock forms in the front of my mind. 'No. Not currently,' I tell her. The ache of longing in my chest as I say that catches me by surprise.

'But there is someone important to you. I can sense it.'

'I'm sorry?'

'When I asked the question, a wistful expression crossed your face. Most people wouldn't spot it, but I'm a professional. That makes me think you have unfinished business with someone.'

I feel a little uncomfortable under her gaze. Although I've

been busy, Jock has been on my mind a lot. I haven't heard from him and, although I did think about texting him a couple of times, I don't want to come across as clingy if he's moving on with his life. Raquel is looking at me expectantly.

'It's definitely finished,' I tell her, before turning to chat to Rosa in Spanish. I make a mental note to stay as far away from Raquel as possible for the duration of her stay. If Jock has moved on, I need to do that as well, and being psychoanalysed by her all the time is not going to help.

14

I'm on my way to the airport again and relishing the time on my own. It's been a tricky few days. Chris and Tim have been, in my view, as good as their word, laying miles of cabling throughout the house and garden while taking care to hide it as discreetly as possible. Rosa doesn't see it that way though, and I'm sure there are hostage negotiations that have required less diplomacy than I've had to exercise to keep everyone happy. However, remote-controlled cameras that can pan, tilt and zoom have now been installed in the reception rooms, the terrace, the garden and by the pool. In addition to them, there are also fixed cameras in all the hallways, apparently to capture any nocturnal corridor creeping. The only place the contestants will be unobserved is when they're in their bedrooms, but even then there are mobile cameras that Chris and Tim can use for any 'morning after the night before' interviews.

I'm collecting six people off two flights from London and Birmingham. Gus is coming out later to swap his minibus for an undamaged one and meet the remaining four from Manchester and Edinburgh. He's printed out signs with the contestants' names for me to hold so, after parking the minibus, I join the group of drivers in the arrivals hall and it's not long before my first contestant emerges.

'Hi, welcome to Mallorca,' I greet the rather frayed-looking man who has marched up to me. 'I'm Beatrice and I'll be looking after you. Can I take your name?'

'Yeah, Jason. Jason Roff.'

'Nice to meet you, Jason. Are you excited about the show?'

'Not really,' he admits. 'The timing couldn't be worse, if I'm honest. I'm right in the middle of a complex deal, so I hope there's good mobile coverage and Wi-Fi, otherwise I'll be on the next flight home.'

He buries his nose in his phone, indicating that the conversation is over, so I turn my attention to looking for the other people I'm supposed to be meeting off this flight. Next to emerge is a heavily made-up young woman called Flo who informs me that she's an influencer with gazillions of followers. Jason is patently unimpressed by her, especially when she asks him to take photos on her phone while she poses with her luggage.

'I've got more important things to do than take your bloody holiday snaps,' he tells her crossly.

'Here, give it to me,' I offer. She's looking mutinous and I'm concerned that things might escalate quickly if I don't step in.

'You know what his problem is?' she observes pointedly as she hands me the phone. 'Small dick energy.'

'You know what your problem is?' he counters. 'Fuck all between your ears.'

'Enough,' I tell them both firmly while silently praying that they aren't one of Raquel's matches. They'd murder each other within five minutes if left unsupervised.

By the time the final contestant from the second flight makes their way over, a little over an hour later, Jason is fidgeting impatiently and Flo is watching him with an expression of disdain.

'Right, follow me to the minibus,' I tell the group of four women and two men. 'It's only about a half-hour drive to the villa, but Gus, our producer, wants to film you arriving individually, so there might be a bit of waiting around when we first get there. I hope that's OK.'

'Fuck's sake,' Jason mutters stroppily. I do hope he's going to lighten up soon, because he's doing a brilliant job of killing the vibe so far. The atmosphere on the journey is subdued; Jason jumped straight into the front passenger seat, which I'm trying hard not to be irritated about. It's not just that he didn't bother to ask any of the others if they wanted it; it's also that there's plenty of space for six in the back seats and I'd be much more comfortable without him brooding next to me. I make a note to bring a large bag or something to block off the front seats on future journeys. Behind me, the women are chatting quietly and the other man is staring out of the window.

'Here we are,' I say as brightly as I can when we pull up at the gates of Villa Madrigal and I enter the access code to let us in.

'Where's the house?' Jason asks.

'Just a few minutes down the track. It's worth the wait, I promise.'

'I'll be the judge of that.'

I'm pleased to see Jason's mood does improve a little when he catches sight of the villa. As arranged with Gus, I pull the minibus round to the side and park it in the space outside my annexe, where Dom is waiting for us.

'Hi, everyone,' he says brightly as we climb out. 'Welcome to Villa Madrigal and *Too Busy for Love*. I trust you all had good journeys?'

'Look, no offence, mate,' Jason begins, 'but I need to crack on. Can you just show me my room and give me the Wi-Fi code?'

I have to stifle a giggle as I can see Flo parodying him out of the corner of my eye.

Dom looks confused. 'Didn't you read the schedule I sent you?'

'No. I've got a lot on right now. I haven't had time to read all that stuff you sent. There was loads of it. You need to learn to summarise, mate.'

'I see. Has everyone else read it?'

'I have,' Flo replies eagerly, flashing Dom a megawatt smile that I suspect is mainly designed to irritate Jason. The sheepish looks from the rest of the group indicate that she's the only one, though.

'Fine,' Dom says a little tetchily. 'I'll take you through it. First of all, we're going to film you walking up to the front door, one by one, with your luggage. When you get inside, your bags will be taken to your rooms but you are to make your way out to the terrace at the back, where welcome drinks have been laid out. Help yourself to a drink and get to know your fellow contestants. For all you know, the person you're destined to spend the rest of your life with is standing right next to you.'

'Look,' Jason counters, 'I know you've got a job to do and everything, but can we do this later? I've got some important calls I need to make.'

'No,' Dom tells him firmly. 'If you'd bothered to read the schedule, you'd see that there are allocated times when you can work, and times when you have to be downstairs and sociable. It's Sunday today; I'm sure whatever it is can wait. I trust you've all read and understand the social media and Wi-Fi policies, at least?'

Even Flo doesn't admit to this one, and Dom sighs deeply.

'You are not to post anything on social media about the show or any of the other contestants. You may upload pictures of the house as long as there are no people in the background, and you can take and upload solo selfies. The Wi-Fi will be unavailable between midnight and six in the morning, as the production team need maximum bandwidth during that time to upload each day's footage to the servers in London, ready for the HQ team to edit it in time to be broadcast the following evening. Any questions?'

Jason looks mutinous but says nothing, so Dom pulls out his walkie-talkie. A quick conversation reveals that Chris and Tim are ready to film the arrivals, so I slip through the door of my annexe and make my way through the house to the hallway to help Rosa with the bags.

* * *

We may only be a day in, but I'm starting to wonder if the concept of this show is seriously flawed. Our initial ten all met each other yesterday but, apart from a bit of posturing from the men, they haven't shown any interest in each other at all. The conversation over the sumptuous dinner that Rosa provided last night was somewhere between stilted and non-existent, and they've pretty much ignored each other all day today, even during the times when they're supposed to be downstairs and socialising. I can tell Gus isn't happy; early this afternoon, he summoned Raquel into the library, which has been re-purposed as Chris and Tim's control room after their plan to use the games room was derailed when Rosa flatly refused to allow them to move the snooker table. They were in there for quite a while and Raquel looked distinctly rattled when she finally emerged. Two 'couples' have been designated to have romantic dinners apart from the group tonight, but there was a noticeable lack of enthusiasm when the pairs were announced at the pre-dinner drinks. I was grateful to see that Flo and Jason weren't paired up, but Raquel is busily coaching the selected four in the hope that they'll actually start to up their game a little. Gus and Dom have scheduled an early morning meeting for the whole group after breakfast, probably to read them the riot act.

'I want you to serve both of the date-night tables,' Gus tells me as the contestants make their way to dinner. 'I know I originally said Rosa could do one, but you're much more photogenic than her and you speak English.'

'Fine. I'll let Rosa know.'

'Thanks.'

The prospect of remaining safely behind her pass and not having to serve the guests absolutely delights Rosa, who didn't take it particularly well when one of the contestants threw a hissy fit at lunchtime because the *Calamari à la Plancha* had tentacles in it. Even though everyone else adored the food and I relayed their comments in full, it's the calamari incident that's stuck in her mind. I'm chatting to her and trying to cheer her up when Raquel bursts in.

'I can't find the Prosecco,' she complains. 'Gus and Dom want the date-night couples to have Prosecco and I can't see it anywhere.'

'It's not out there,' I tell her calmly. 'Wait here and I'll get you a bottle.'

Rosa has made it very clear that the only person she will tolerate in her kitchen besides her and her assistant is me. Everyone else is to stay well clear, so I can see her twitching at Raquel's presence, even though she's on the other side of the pass. I hastily retrieve a bottle of Prosecco from one of the fridges and give it to Raquel, who dashes outside with it.

'Taste this,' Rosa instructs me, holding out a spoon with a prawn and some sauce in it. I gently take it from her and pop it in my mouth.

'What do you think?' she asks.

'It's incredible. What is it?'

'*Zarzuela de Pescado y Mariscos*. It originates from Barcelona. I'm serving it to the date-night couples with fried potatoes and salad.'

Our conversation is cut short by a hiss and a crackle from my walkie-talkie. I'm not a fan of it as it keeps making me jump, but Gus insisted we had them.

'Date-night tables are ready for their first course,' his tinny voice says.

'On my way,' I tell him. Rosa starts plating up and, as soon as the food for the first table is ready, I load it onto a tray and carry it outside. At the buffet, the guests are busily loading up their plates and I'm glad to see that they are at least talking to each other now. The date-night tables are further away in secluded areas of the garden so I concentrate on my feet; tripping over with a tray of food is not going to endear me to anyone.

I haven't been to the date-night tables in the darkness before, and I have to say they do look magical. As well as the obligatory fairy lights draped around, there are also candles in storm lanterns hanging on special brackets. The electric lighting, important for the filming, is carefully concealed and softened to prevent any harsh shadows from being cast. It reminds me a little of the pub that Jock and I went to on our last night together, and it's all I can do to force the bittersweet memory out of my mind and concentrate on the here and now.

'Good evening,' I say to Marcus and Deborah, who I'm pleased to see are chatting quietly to each other and looking fairly relaxed. 'I have your first course here. It's a traditional

Spanish fish stew, served with fried potatoes and salad.' As I'm speaking, I lay the various plates in front of them, taking care to serve them from the left so as not to block the view of the camera that is out there in the darkness somewhere. '¡Buen provecho!' I add as I carefully pick up the tray and retreat.

'Well done,' Gus says encouragingly when I return to the villa after serving the second table. 'You looked completely natural and remembered the sightlines. At least someone round here is listening to me.'

Rosa is also in a good mood when I walk back into the kitchen and, for the first time since the crew arrived, everyone seems happy. Well, everyone except Raquel, who I spotted in the sitting room morosely nursing a glass of wine the size of a fishbowl. For a moment, I'm tempted to go in and check whether she's all right, but then I remember her eagerness to delve into my private life and decide against it. I'm struggling enough with Jock popping into my mind, without her encouraging it.

15

It's Wednesday morning and the first show went out last night. I haven't seen it, because I was flat out serving dinner and helping to clear up when it was on, but the list of unread messages on my phone when I woke up indicate that a good number of people who know me must have watched it. In amongst the good wishes, I'm surprised to see a message from Jock.

> I just saw you on Too Busy for Love. Can you confirm rumours that you're TV's hottest waitress now?

I grin as I type out a reply. I'm stupidly pleased to hear from him.

> I don't know about that, but it's interesting work and I'm enjoying it. How come you have time to be watching TV?

I watch the screen for a while but the ticks stay resolutely grey. He must be working.

* * *

'Beatrice, can I borrow you for five minutes as soon as you get some down time?' Gus asks as I'm carrying the breakfast buffet dishes outside. His face is serious.

'Sure. Let me just get this stuff out and then I'll come to the control room. I'll be with you in a second.'

My promise is slightly derailed by the fact that Flo has absent-mindedly helped herself to the soya milk rather than the regular milk, so I have to take it back into the kitchen and top it up.

'Come in,' Gus's voice calls when I tap on the door. I'm surprised to see that he's alone; the techies seem to pretty much live in here, so I was expecting to see them hunched over their desks as usual.

'Have a seat.' He indicates the chair that Chris usually occupies, while settling himself in Tim's chair.

'What's up?'

'Tell me about your previous job.'

'What do you mean?'

'You said in the interview that you were looking for a new challenge, but there's more to it than that, isn't there? It's come to my attention that you left out some fairly pertinent information. Why?'

I sigh. I should have known this was going to catch up with me. Even thousands of miles away, Hotel Dufour is still managing to poison my life.

'Look, I didn't know what was going on, I promise. The police investigated and cleared me of everything. When is this ever going to bloody end?'

'I sympathise. However, it creates a problem for us because someone has recognised you on social media and there's a bit of a feeding frenzy going on. You know what it's like when the trolls think they've got hold of a juicy titbit.'

'I don't. What do you mean by feeding frenzy?' I pull out my phone and launch X, entering the name of the show in the search box.

'Are you sure you want to do that?' Gus asks. 'Some of it is vicious.'

'I need to know what people are saying.' I regret my words almost as soon as the screen loads and I see what he's talking about. Someone has posted the picture of me and Jock outside the hotel, with a screengrab of me serving dinner last night next to it. The caption underneath reads:

Look where the brothel girl is! If the contestants on Too Busy for Love don't fancy getting it on with each other, I'm sure she'll help out.

That's bad enough, but the comments underneath are ten times worse. I can feel the blood draining from my face as I read. How can people write such disgusting things about someone they've never met and know nothing about? There are a number that explicitly detail various depraved acts they would either like to carry out on me, or have me carry out on them. It's too much and I'm aware that tears are pouring down my face.

'Are you all right?' Gus asks gently. 'Do you want some water or something?'

'Please.'

'Stay there. Don't move and don't look at your phone any more.' He gingerly removes my phone from my grasp, placing it on the table before leaving the room. I stare at it while he's gone; the screen is dark now, but I'm very aware of the torrent of abuse it's just served up to me. I'm shivering violently when Gus returns a few moments later with a bottle of water, which he hands to me. I just about manage to grip it, but my hands are shaking so much that undoing the lid proves impossible.

'Give it to me,' he suggests, gently prising it out of my grip and loosening the top for me, before holding it to my lips. I suck down the cool, soothing liquid greedily.

'Gently,' he chides. 'You've had a shock, and there's a risk it will all come straight back up if you overdo it.'

When the bottle is half empty, he takes it away and screws the lid back on. 'You can have some more in a minute,' he tells me. 'Let's just see how that settles first, shall we?'

There's a knock on the door and Rosa appears. As soon as she spots me, her expression changes completely; she rushes over and wraps her arms around me.

'Beatrice, what on earth is the matter?' she fusses in rapid Spanish. 'Are you unwell? Do you want me to get Pedro to take you to the doctor?'

'I'm not unwell,' I tell her shakily. 'I've just had some shocking news.'

'Why don't I take you to your room for a lie-down. You're in no fit state to work.'

'Thank you, Rosa, but I need to talk to Gus. I'll be OK.'

'If you need anything, anything at all...'

'Thank you, Rosa.'

'I won't pretend to have understood a word of that,' Gus observes once Rosa has left the room, 'but she clearly has a lot of affection for you. How are you feeling now?'

'A little better, I think.'

'Good. There are some really important things I need you to hear. Are you listening to me?'

'Yes.'

'Number one. It's horrible and disgusting, and the people

who wrote it should be ashamed of themselves, but you're not in any danger. These people are just keyboard warriors, impotently pouring their rage out at anyone and everyone. They're not coming for you; they never are. If they met you in the street, they'd probably run away. Have you heard me?'

'Did you see what they wrote?' I ask him incredulously.

'I did. But this is the second thing I need you to hear. You are not alone. I guarantee you that pretty much every woman who has even the smallest public profile has had this kind of abuse directed at them. It will be of little comfort to you, but I've seen much worse. They're not targeting you specifically, you just happen to have caught their eye today. They'll move on.'

'Of course they're fucking targeting me,' I snarl suddenly. 'They're not threatening to do those things to you, are they?'

'No,' he admits. 'It's a mainly misogynistic hate crime. But I know countless women in our industry that it's happened to, and I can promise you that, although it's equally upsetting for them, nobody has harmed them.'

Our conversation is interrupted by Dom bursting in. 'Hold the firing squad,' he announces. 'Something extraordinary is happening.'

Firing squad?

'What is it?' Gus asks.

'OK, so live viewing figures for last night's show were disappointing, as you know. But it seems the Beatrice situation is stoking interest and the online figures are climbing through the roof. She might just be our ticket out of trouble.'

'Were you going to fire me?' I ask in disbelief.

'One at a time. Jeez, let me think.'

'Oh my God. You were! All that mister nice guy stuff was just an act. You're unbelievable.' I start to get to my feet.

'I wasn't going to fire you,' Gus says firmly enough to stop me leaving the room. 'But I was going to reassign you, I admit.'

'What does that mean?'

'I was going to take you away from front-line duties and keep you in the background, helping Rosa and translating.'

'Yeah, about that. I have an idea,' Dom interjects. 'What if we didn't do that? We're hanging by a thread here. If we don't pull a rabbit out of this shitty hat soon, HQ is going to shut us down.'

This is also news to me. 'What do you mean, "shut us down"?'

'Dom's right,' Gus sighs. 'Not only were the viewing figures poor, but the reviews were terrible. People are saying there's no chemistry and that it all feels so fake, we're probably not even in Mallorca. We've been given until the end of the week to turn it around, otherwise they're pulling the plug.'

'So here's my idea,' Dom says enthusiastically. 'Normally, we'd do exactly what Gus is suggesting. We'd whip you out of the limelight, probably fire you, issue some statement along the lines of "we had no idea but she's gone now, sorry everyone," and hope that resolved it. But what if we took all this and used it to our advantage? Give Beatrice more screen time, not less, and give her the opportunity to call out her abusers.'

'Wouldn't that just be stoking the fire?' I ask tentatively. 'I don't want this to get any worse.'

'What were you thinking?' Gus prompts, ignoring me.

'Flo,' Dom replies simply. 'She's got loads of experience of being trolled, so she'd be a great person for Beatrice to talk to. We engineer a conversation on camera, where Beatrice talks to Flo about what's happened, maybe shows her some of the comments, and we make a thing about it. Start a conversation about the damage this stuff does to people.'

'I'm not sure HQ would like us going off-piste like that,' Gus tells him.

'HQ want good viewing figures and reviews. I don't think they care beyond that.'

'Even if we shoot it, there's no guarantee they won't cut it. It'll probably be a waste of time.'

'Then we call them and sell them the idea. We need to do something, and this might be good for both Beatrice and the show. Let's talk about something that bloody matters for once, rather than our usual "celebrities being absolutely hopeless at ordinary life tasks" bollocks.'

'Fine. You sell it, and you go under the bus if they hate it. Still want to do it?'

'Yup. What about you, Beatrice? Are you up for it?'

'I'm still not entirely sure what the plan is,' I admit. 'But if it gives me an opportunity to tell my side of the story, I'm in.'

'Right,' Gus declares. 'We're doing this. Beatrice, if you need to take a couple of hours away to recover, we'll cope without you. Remember, even if HQ goes for it and we film it today, it won't screen until tomorrow night, so don't expect anything to change immediately. Try not to look at your social media for a while, OK? It won't do you any good.'

As soon as I'm dismissed, I practically sprint to my annexe, where I rip off all my clothes and stuff them in the dirty clothes bin, before spending as long as I dare under the hottest shower I can bear. I know Gus is right and I'm not unique, but it doesn't stop me feeling violated. I just hope their plan works.

16

I wasn't sure about Dom's idea, but it turned out to be brilliant. We filmed a segment where I was behind the pool bar and Flo came over to get a drink. She asked if I was OK, and that got the conversation going and gave me the opportunity to explain my role at Hotel Dufour and show her the comments on my phone. Not only did she reassure me, but she called out some of my trolls by name on camera, which I thought was incredibly brave of her. There was an outpouring of love after the episode aired and, although there are still a few people making nasty comments, most of the remarks about me online are now fairly positive. Gus is also pleased, as the ratings and audience numbers soared almost overnight, and have stayed up during the weeks since. Apparently, the viewers loved the fact that we tackled such a corrosive issue head-on.

Jock sent another message asking if I was all right after the show aired, and we ended up having a bit of back and forth, which cheered me up immensely. He told me he's working at a restaurant in Glasgow called Gregory's and is really enjoying it. The menu is very much British, which he said is a huge relief after Madame's French obsession. I did search online for the restaurant but came up blank. When I questioned him about it, he said the owners were old school and didn't feel an online presence was necessary. After that brief flurry, the messages died down again, which is probably just as well, because talking to him just makes me realise how much I miss him.

The person who has turned out to be a total star is Flo. Dom wasn't lying when he said she'd had her fair share of trolls; some of the stuff she showed me that they'd said about her was breathtakingly vile. However, her determination not to allow herself to be affected by it has really helped me, and she's very sweetly accompanied me on every airport run so I'm not on my own. Her compassion has done her no harm, as she showed me a serious bump in the number of people following her online after our chat. She's also the only one of the original contestants left. Jason was axed in the first replacement, which came as a surprise to nobody as he remained totally self-absorbed and pretty much ignored the other contestants for the entire time he was with us. I think he was just as relieved to leave as we were to see the back of him. I'm not really sure why he applied for the show in the first place. It wasn't long before the only three left out of the original ten were Flo, Marcus and Deborah.

Marcus and Deborah have been the golden couple since day one, but Marcus managed to depth charge that a couple of nights ago when he had a few too many glasses of wine and foolishly admitted to one of the other men that he and Deborah didn't fancy each other at all and were faking it to get the prize money. The microphone picked it up, naturally, and that was the end of them. Their place in the limelight has been taken by Flo and Rob. Rob's a self-employed plumber who arrived in week three, and they've been absolutely smitten with each other from the moment they met.

'Do you think we should go all the way?' she asks me. We're sitting at a table in one of the cafés in the arrivals hall, having dumped Marcus and Deborah in the check-in queue. Our final two contestants are on the inbound flight, which the board informs me should be landing in just under an hour.

'Do you want to?'

'I don't not want to, but it feels a bit weird knowing that millions of people will be watching.'

'They're not going to see you actually having sex, Flo. Not unless you decide to do it on camera, anyway.'

'No, but they'll know that we have. My mum watches the show.'

'Mm. I get your point.'

'It's stupid, isn't it. I'm a grown woman; I should be free to have sex with whoever I want.'

'Do you think you'll take your relationship into the outside world?'

'I don't know. Rob would really like to, but I wonder whether it would survive outside this bubble. It's easy for us in here; he can't exactly work, unless the sink gets blocked or something, and, apart from a few selfies to keep my followers onside, neither can I. So we've got all the time in the world to lie by the pool and chat. But it won't be like that back home, and I'm not sure he understands how busy I am. I need to be creating high-quality content pretty much every day, otherwise my followers will lose interest and so will the brands. I've also got to keep on top of my social media. It sounds like a dream life, but I'm regularly working until midnight. I'm lucky, because being in here keeps my profile high, but I know I'm going to have to hit the ground running when I get home.'

'Have you talked to him about how you feel?'

'You're sounding like Raquel.' She giggles. 'I have, but I don't think he gets it. I'm not sure he sees what I do as work. To him, my life is easy. Couple of selfies with a Starbucks in the morning before taking the rest of the day off or going shopping, that's what he thinks. What are you going to do after this? Are the TV company whisking you off to another exotic location?'

'I don't know. They haven't said anything. I'd like to think they're pleased with my work, but I reckon the fact that I wasn't totally up front about Hotel Dufour has left a slightly bitter taste in their mouths. Who knows?'

'You seem pretty chilled about it.'

'I am.' This isn't strictly true. Although the pay here is good and I haven't had any living expenses, so it's not strictly the end of the world if I don't get work straight away, the idea of going back to Ludlow fills me with dread. I've also never had a fixed-term contract before and I'm not sure what I'm supposed to do when it ends. On the one hand, there's nothing stopping me from getting in touch with the agency to see what they've got coming up, but I don't want to miss out on another contract with Caster-bridge Media if they're planning to offer one. I've been trying to find a way to broach the subject with Gus, but the opportunity hasn't presented itself so far.

'Who are we picking up?' Flo asks a few minutes later. 'Give me the deets.'

'We've got a woman called Abby, who is the director of a construction company based in Leeds, and a guy called James who has his own wine business called The Online Sommelier.'

'So we're looking for a woman in a hard hat and a wino.'

'Let me know when you spot them,' I reply with a smile.

* * *

I don't know who fits Flo's stereotypes less well. I knew Abby wouldn't be wearing a hard hat, obviously, but I was expecting someone who looked like they worked in construction, so the petite woman with long chestnut hair and wide hazel eyes who approaches us catches me by surprise. James must be well over six foot as he towers over the rest of us. He's obviously a man who takes pride in his appearance, as he's immaculately turned out.

'I wondered if you were the other contestant when I saw you at the boarding gate,' Abby says to him as we head out of the airport complex onto the dual carriageway.

'I had you clocked pretty much straight away,' he replies. I catch Flo's eye and we both smile. They're like chalk and cheese to listen to. Where Abby's accent is clearly northern, James has the kind of posh-boy drawl that makes you think of private jets, yachts and horse racing.

'What gave me away?' Abby asks.

'Simple. Mallorca is a holiday destination, so a young woman travelling alone stuck out among the families and couples.'

'Very good, Detective. I could have been a local returning home, though. Did you think of that?'

'I did, but I ruled it out almost straight away.'

'Why?'

'Don't take this the wrong way, but you don't give off a Hispanic vibe. What do you do, by the way?'

'I'm sorry?'

'I was just wondering how someone like you could be too busy for love. I would have thought you would have men queueing round the block.'

'Flatterer. I'm in construction. I spend most of my time either stuck in an office or dressed in safety gear on site, and that's not a look that most men are going to queue up for.'

'Sounds intriguing.'

Abby laughs. 'It really isn't. What about you, what do you do?'

'I'm in the wine trade.'

'What, like an off-licence?'

'Not exactly. My customers are not the kind of people who would buy wine from the off-licence. They're connoisseurs who expect the very best and are prepared to pay handsomely for it. My job is to find exceptional wines for them.'

'When you say "pay handsomely"...'

'I'll give you an example. One of my clients asked me to track down a case of 1998 Château Petrus for him last week. It wasn't a hard wine to find, but it is at the upper end, price wise. Do you know much about wine?'

'I know I like a good Shiraz, but I don't normally spend more than a tenner on a bottle of wine. How much is Petrus?'

'Four and a half thousand pounds a bottle for the 1998.'

'Fuck me.'

'That's not the best bit. My client bought six for a dinner party he was hosting. He described it to me as "nothing outlandish, just a few close friends coming round for the evening". It's a different world, but it makes life interesting. What sort of construction do you do?'

'Residential.'

Although I did find James's wine story moderately interesting, construction totally isn't my thing so I tune them out and chat to Flo until Abby suddenly leans forward. 'Beatrice, did you know you're famous back home?'

'Really?' I try to keep my voice neutral.

'Yeah. I've been watching the show and following it on social media, obviously, and you've got a lot of fans, particularly among the female viewers. You and Flo are like the poster girls of the anti-misogyny revolution.' I glance across at Flo, who beams at me.

'The woman you worked for, what was her name?' Abby
continues after a moment.

'I knew her as Madame Dufour, but I think her real name is
Eileen Strickland.'

'That's the one. She just got sent to prison, did you see?'

'No. We can get UK news at the villa, but I haven't been
following it.'

'There's bound to be something online. Have a look.'

As soon as we get to the villa, Flo dashes off to find Rob while
Gus talks Abby and James through the arrivals process, so I take
the opportunity to check the internet. It takes a little while as it's
buried in the minor news and the article is short, but I read it
with interest.

> Eileen Strickland, the owner of the notorious brothel Hotel
> Dufour, was today sentenced to 14 years imprisonment at the
> central criminal court after being found guilty under section 33
> of the Sexual Offences Act for keeping a brothel, section 53 of
> the same act for controlling prostitution for gain, and sections
> 2 and 3 of the Modern Slavery Act for trafficking and sexual
> exploitation. Her daughter, Maria Strickland, was also
> sentenced to 7 years for controlling prostitution for gain. In his
> summing up, Richard Stevens KC described them as
> 'depraved individuals who remorselessly preyed on vulnerable
> young women with the sole intention of lining their own pock-
> ets,' adding, 'society will be much improved without you in it.'

I'm assuming Jock hasn't seen it either as I'm sure he would
have told me, so I screenshot it and send it to him. He must be
working as he doesn't reply, so I go to help Rosa with the dinner.
As I'm carrying the trays out to the date-night tables, I notice that
Abby and James are sitting opposite each other at the main table,

deep in conversation. I can't help smiling as I contemplate the physical differences between them. If they become a couple, she's either going to have to saw his legs off at the knees or get a stool, otherwise kissing is going to be very challenging. Flo and Rob are also having a heart to heart and, by the eager look on his face, I'm surmising that Flo has decided to take things to the next level, even if her mum is watching.

The only problem with these budding romances happening all around me is that they throw my own situation into sharp relief, and that inevitably turns my mind back to Jock. When I check my phone just before going to bed, I can see that he's replied to my message.

> They obviously caught Maria in the act then.
> Good.

I haven't told Jock that I contacted DI Winter and shared what Maria had told us. As I climb into bed and turn off the light, I try to work out whether I should. In the end, I decide to leave it; it's not important and, nice as it is to hear from him, I need to focus on the fact that my contract is coming to an end soon and start to make a plan about what to do next. It's difficult though, and I find myself trying to picture him in his new role. Does he miss me the same way as I miss him, or does he see me purely as a friend who shared a bizarre week in London with him?

17

'You have got to be bloody kidding me. What reason did they give?' Abby says crossly into her phone.

I'm walking down to restock the pool bar and she's lying on a sun lounger. I'm not at all surprised to see James stretched out on the lounger next to hers, his long limbs pale in the sunlight.

'All is not well in the world of construction this morning,' he offers quietly by way of explanation when he sees me.

'No, it's fine, Ella,' Abby continues after a moment or two. 'We'll just have to go to plan B and see if we can change their minds that way. It's not ideal, but we don't really have any other choice. Yes, thanks for letting me know. All right, yeah. Bye.'

'Bollocks,' she says vehemently as she slams her phone down on the table.

'Are you OK?' I ask. 'I couldn't help overhearing.'

'Not really. Fucking Thanet Borough Council have turned down my planning permission application, which means Dad's probably going to be on the phone to roast my arse any moment now.'

'How come?' James asks, propping himself up on one arm so he can look at her.

'Dad's business model is simple and he likes to stick to it. He buys patches of land that have planning permission but are too small for the big developers to bother with, and builds on them. It's a good model, but I thought we were missing a trick.'

'What kind of trick?'

'Redevelopment. I've got nothing against new builds, but I reckon we've been missing out on a big opportunity. Look at all those warehouses in the east end of London, for example. Somebody bought them, probably for a song, converted them into flats and made a killing. I want a slice of that action.'

'So you bought a warehouse?' I ask.

'They're all gone now – the good ones, anyway. No, I found this shitty old hotel in Margate that was coming up for auction. It was last owned by one of the budget chains, but I think they used it during the pandemic as accommodation for the homeless, who made a bit of a mess in there. They obviously felt it wasn't worth spending the money needed to bring it back up to scratch afterwards, so they decided to close it and sell it off.'

'Doesn't sound very promising,' James observes. 'Why Margate? It's a dump, isn't it?'

'No. There are some seedy bits of it, but it's up and coming in a big way. For starters, it's got a whole artistic scene going on. It's Tracey Emin's home town and you've got the Turner contemporary art gallery, as well as the Antony Gormley 'Another Time' sculpture. And, despite being a mess inside, the hotel building itself is a classic example of Art Deco architecture with fabulous views down to the sea.'

'What was your plan?' I ask.

'Simple. Restore the exterior to its former glory and convert the interior into luxury apartments.'

'Seems like a sensible idea,' I observe. 'Why aren't the borough council keen?'

'Apparently, there have been objections from some people who feel that it's an important local landmark and converting it into flats is tantamount to sacrilege. They've lobbied the council and the council have listened to them over the greedy developer.'

'I heard you mention a plan B though, so you were obviously prepared for this eventuality.'

'There is a plan B, but it's not going to be good for us or the council.'

'What is it?'

'We mothball the place. It's already boarded up so we just let it decay. Eventually, it will either fall down or the council will give in.'

'A war of attrition,' James observes.

'Yup, and it pretty much guarantees we will automatically get turned down for anything we want to do in that area in future, but it's basically the only card we can play now.'

'Can't you sell it?' I ask.

'Who's going to buy it? It's obviously not viable as a hotel, otherwise the chain wouldn't have closed it, and you can't convert it into anything else because the council won't let you. It's a white elephant, as Dad will take delight in pointing out when he calls to give me a large helping of "I told you so" with a generous dash of "this is why we do it my way" on the side.'

'He sounds a bit of a tyrant, if you don't mind me saying,' James tells her. 'He should be proud that you're looking for new opportunities.'

'He really isn't a tyrant. He's actually very supportive of me, generally. Even though he didn't like this idea, he let me run with it. That's the kind of person he is. Having said that, I went against his advice and it hasn't paid off. The schadenfreude will be too great for him to resist.'

As if on cue, her phone rings again and she groans. 'Here we go. Hi, Dad. Yes, Ella just phoned me...'

She gets up from the sun lounger and wanders away, evidently wanting to be out of earshot for the conversation with her father. James watches her go with a strange expression on his face.

'Are you OK there?' I ask.

'Oh. Yes, umm, sorry. I was miles away for a moment.'

'Dare I ask if it has anything to do with Abby?'

'Mm. Have you heard the phrase "Hate to see you go, love to watch you leave"?'

'No. What does it – oh!' I tell him as the penny drops.

'Doesn't she have a magnificent rump?' he says wistfully, gazing down to Abby, who is striding back and forth in her bikini at the far end of the pool, evidently having quite a forceful conversation, if her facial expression and hand gestures are anything to go by.

'She's not a cow, James! If I may offer you some advice, talking about women like they're slabs of meat is unlikely to get you the result you want.'

'How would you describe it then? "Nice arse" just sounds common.'

'Why don't you focus on her as a whole, rather than picking on a single bodily feature?'

'I'm not sure I follow. Surely I'm allowed to admire her physique?'

'Of course you are, but it has to be in the context of her as a person. If you make remarks about it in isolation, that's not attractive.'

'Are you telling me that women don't like men to find them beautiful?'

'Of course we do! But we want to be found beautiful as people, not just as a set of physical attributes. Does that make sense?'

'But I don't know that much about her as a person yet. I can only judge what I see.'

'Then learn. Let's translate this into your world. What was that wine you were talking about on the way from the airport?'

'Château Petrus.'

'That's the one. So, imagine you've bought a bottle of that and you've invited me round to taste it with you.'

'Not very realistic. I may get it for customers but it's way out of my price range.'

'You've won the lottery.'

'Oh, OK.'

'So, you're all excited about sharing this incredible wine, right?'

He smiles. 'If it's Château Petrus, I'm not sure I'm sharing it.'

'You're sharing it,' I tell him firmly. 'You pour two glasses, and you do the whole swirling and sniffing thing before taking a taste and telling me all the things I should be able to pick up. Then I take a mouthful, swallow it straight down and tell you, "It's all right, I suppose, but I prefer rosé". How do you feel?'

'I'd take it off you and probably never speak to you again.'

'But that's exactly what you're doing to Abby, don't you see? She's every bit as complex as your Château Petrus, but all you're talking about is the shape of the bottle. How would you describe her if she was a wine?'

'The first thing I'd look at in a fine wine is the appearance. Its colour and opacity.'

'OK. I think we can both agree you've done that with Abby. What comes next?'

'Then I'd smell the wine, to get the top note aromas. Primary aromas from the grape varietal and secondary aromas from the maturing process – what kind of barrels it's been aged in, for example.'

'And if Abby were a wine, what aromas would you expect to smell?'

He looks over at Abby, who is still striding back and forth, talking animatedly into her phone.

'Floral top notes, but there's spice in there too, with an earthy undercurrent. Complex, but not unapproachably so.'

'Now we're getting somewhere. Tell me how you came to use those words.'

'The floral top notes because she's very feminine.'

'That's to be expected, given that she's a woman.'

'You know what I mean. She has a delicate and very feminine physique.'

'You're in danger of going purely on appearances again there, James.'

'Ah, but then you pick up the spice. It's the exotic, heady clash between the floral top notes and the fact that she works in a very unfeminine industry. It's intriguing, unusual, and makes you want to find out more.'

'And the earthy undercurrent?'

He laughs. '"Bollocks." "Fucking Thanet Borough Council." "Roast my arse." Those aren't the words of a fragile princess. She's definitely got her feet on the ground. I've never met anybody like her. She's utterly mesmerising.'

'So I think we can agree there's a lot more to her than just her "rump", as you put it. Do you want me to have a chat with Raquel, to see if she can pair you up for a date night?'

'Would you? That would be amazing.'

'I can't promise anything, but I'll put a word in. Ah, it looks like the roasting is done.'

'How did you get on?' James asks Abby as she rejoins us, taking her place on the sun lounger once more.

'It was as I predicted. What pisses me off is that it's happened on the first one, which means it's going to be much harder to persuade him to take the risk again. Thankfully, we've just sold the last plot on one of our developments in Ashford, so our cash-flow position is strong and we can afford the hit. It's just such a bloody waste of a fabulous opportunity.'

'Can't you appeal against the decision?' James asks.

'We were talking about that. We are going to appeal, but there's no guarantee it will make a difference, and who knows how long it will take. In the meantime, we'll mothball it and let nature take its course. The residents might not be so hoity-bloody-toity when it's a graffiti-covered, crumbling eyesore.'

My curiosity gets the better of me. 'Have you got any pictures?' I ask her.

'Oh yeah, loads. Hang on.' She picks up her phone and launches an app, navigating through folders until she comes to the one she's looking for. 'Here you go.' She holds the phone out to me. As I scroll through the pictures of the hotel, I can immediately see why she was attracted to it. It's definitely seen better days but it's still a beautiful example of the style. It's a simple, streamlined building that reminds me a little of an old-fashioned cinema. The steel-framed windows either side of the magnificent front door are curved, drawing the eye as if beckoning you inside. If I close my eyes, I can almost picture it in a black and white movie, with a smartly uniformed doorman greeting guests as they step out of their opulent vintage limousines.

'It's gorgeous,' I sigh.

'That's what I thought,' Abby agrees. 'Unfortunately, all the period features inside have been ripped out at some point in its history, so it's indistinguishable from any other building once you go in. I was going to try to recreate some of the original charm though. Hand me back my phone and I'll see if I can find the computer mock-ups of what I had planned.'

After a bit more searching, she finds what she's looking for and hands the phone back to me. I'm aware of James watching over my shoulder as I scroll through the images of the lobby area, floor plans showing the old and new layouts, and a virtual tour through one of the apartments, with panoramic views out over the sea from the large windows.

'The amount of work I put into those sodding windows,' Abby sighs as we look at the screen together. 'How to keep them looking correct but make them thermally efficient at the same time.'

'I don't understand how anyone could object to this,' James murmurs. 'I don't even like Margate, but I'm looking for the "buy it now" button.'

'There's also a car park, which is a rarity for a building of this age,' Abby tells him. 'I suspect the council would have been more amenable if I'd come up with a plan to convert it into affordable housing, because that's the buzzword these days, but it just doesn't suit a building like this. Also, wealthier people spend more, which is good for the local economy.'

'A rising tide lifts all boats,' James observes.

'What's that got to do with it?' Abby asks, nonplussed.

'It's a metaphor for collective benefit. I do well, but you also benefit from my success.'

'I see. Well, if we're going to stick with tidal metaphors then Thanet council are King Canute, trying to stop the waves coming in.'

'Nicely done,' James congratulates her. 'Canute didn't succeed in turning back the tide though, so maybe there's hope for you.'

'It'll take a bloody miracle,' Abby replies despondently, taking her phone back and slumping on her sun lounger.

'*Illegitimi non carborundum*,' James tells her with a smile.

'What's that?'

'Latin. Well, not proper Latin, but it basically means "don't let the bastards grind you down".'

'Don't worry,' she mutters as she tilts her face up to the sun and adjusts her sunglasses. 'I may be down, but I'm far from out.'

Sensing that the conversation is over, I turn my attention back to my original task of restocking the bar. After a few minutes, James wanders over and leans against the counter.

'Can I get you something?' I ask him.

'You know that wine we were talking about earlier?'

'Yes.'

'There's another flavour, on the finish. It's slightly flinty, probably as a result of the soil it's grown in: the *terroir*, as we call it in the business. It's telling you that this is a wine made with confidence, firmly rooted in its environment and unashamed of what it is. A wine that showcases its *terroir* so strongly is truly magical.'

I laugh softly. 'You have got it bad.'

'I think I'm in love,' he says simply.

18

Raquel needed no persuading to put James and Abby forward for a date night, as she'd already noticed that James was keen on Abby, although she wasn't entirely sure his feelings were reciprocated. Abby was duly summoned for interview where, according to what Raquel told me afterwards, she admitted she'd initially dismissed James as a 'posh knob' with whom she had nothing in common. However, despite him being totally not the kind of guy she normally went for, she found him easy to talk to and he was definitely growing on her. I, on the other hand, was summoned to see Gus, who was practically salivating over the footage of my chat with James; annoyingly, I'd forgotten that the whole thing would be recorded. On the plus side, he thinks my 'sage advice', as he put it, will further endear me to the viewers and help to shut down the few remaining trolls. I've been firmly avoiding any social media to do with the show, so I'm happy to take his word for it.

I'm helping Rosa to clear up after lunch when James appears, looking a little nervous.

'What's up?' I ask him.

'You know Abby and I are on a date night tonight?'

'Yes. That's what you wanted, wasn't it?'

'It is, absolutely. But, umm, don't take this the wrong way, I'd like to serve her something a bit more special than the run of the mill wine we normally have. I also thought...' He stops and I notice he's blushing.

'What is it?'

'You might say this is hideously old-fashioned, and you must tell me if it's a stupid idea, but I thought I'd like to get her some flowers.'

'I think that's a lovely idea. Just say what you want and I'll chat to Gus and see what we can get organised for you.'

'Umm, no. I was rather hoping you would help me to get them myself. I'm not sure it's very romantic to give her flowers that someone else has bought on my behalf, do you know what I mean? I noticed you speak Spanish, and I know you drive, so I was hoping I could commandeer you for a couple of hours to take me to the nearest town and translate for me.'

'Goodness, James. I'll have to check with Gus and Rosa, but I don't imagine there will be a problem. Do you know where you want to go?'

'I've already researched the wine, but I'm happy to be guided by you on the best place for flowers.'

* * *

I should have known that buying wine with James wasn't going to be as simple as a trip to a supermarket. We're heading into the mountains to a winery called Bodega Ribas.

'I remembered Abby saying she liked Shiraz,' he tells me excitedly as I negotiate the narrow roads. 'The wine I want to buy is called Ribas de Cabrera. It's only twenty per cent Syrah grapes, with the remaining eighty being Mantonegro, a local grape variety, but it tastes like Shiraz on speed. They only make it when the harvested grapes are of exceptional quality and, get this, they select the grapes for this wine individually.'

'Wow, I bet that doesn't come cheap.'

'It's not as expensive as you might think. Depending on where you get it from, you can pay anything from sixty to eighty pounds a bottle.'

'That's still a hell of a lot, James. I don't want to rain on your parade, but do you think you might be overthinking this, just a little? I'm sure she'd be happy with something a fraction of that price. What if she doesn't like it, or just knocks it back?'

'She might be happy with something cheap, but what does it say about my feelings for her if I skimp on the wine? She's an exceptional woman, and I wouldn't be comfortable serving her anything less than an exceptional wine.'

I give him a brief grin. 'You're the boss.'

I'm relieved to discover that the people at the bodega speak fluent English, so I'm not forced to translate wine-talk. I also should have guessed that James knows the owners, so there's lots of discussion about their various wines and different vintages. A seemingly endless array of bottles is brought in, opened, tasted and discussed at length. I'm also relieved to note that he carefully spits each wine into a container after tasting it; he's never going to impress Abby if he's plastered. We're there for nearly an hour before we finally climb back into the minibus with James cradling his bottle of Cabrera like a baby.

'Right,' I tell him. 'Rosa has recommended a florist not far from the villa, and I'm afraid she's also given me a list of things I need to pick up for her. What sort of flowers are you after? Roses would be the obvious choice.'

'Yeah, but they're terribly clichéd. I don't know what I want exactly, but hopefully I'll spot something when we get there.'

If I thought the visit to the winery was drawn out, the florist is agonising. In the end, I set James and the florist up with a kind of pointing and gesturing system so I can leave them to it and go to get the things on Rosa's list. When I get back to the minibus, he's waiting for me with the largest bouquet I think I've ever seen.

'Goodness,' I exclaim. 'Did you buy the whole shop?'

'It does feel a bit like that,' he admits. 'I couldn't decide, so in the end I asked her to make me a bouquet with a bit of everything.'

'I bet she loved you. I dread to think how much it cost. I just hope Abby appreciates all the effort you've gone to.' I stow Rosa's shopping in the boot while James reverentially lays the bouquet on the floor between the back seats.

'I've just had a thought,' James says suddenly as we drive through the gates of the villa. 'How am I going to smuggle the flowers in without Abby spotting them?'

'Leave them with me,' I tell him. 'I'll take them into my room and store them until you're ready. Do you want me to put them next to your seat so you can give them to her at dinner? I don't think we have a vase big enough, so I might need to put them in a bucket.'

'That would be brilliant, thank you. Do you know if you have any decanters?'

'I would have thought so. I'll ask Rosa for one and bring it to your room.'

'Thanks. The wine is too young to have a sediment but it will still benefit from breathing properly.'

'I'll take your word for it,' I tell him with a smile.

* * *

Rosa is unimpressed by both the flowers, which she dismisses as 'ridiculously extravagant', and the fuss over the wine. 'He's putting too much expectation on the poor woman,' she says with a sniff. 'I saw it a lot when we had the restaurant – men making lavish displays and ordering everything expensive, when it's clear the woman would have preferred something simple. It was good for our profit margin, but for the women? Not so much.'

'I think it's only a problem if he becomes a wine bore over dinner. Nothing is likely to turn her off more than a lecture on top notes and *terroir*.'

'How did you become such an expert all of a sudden?' Rosa asks.

'An hour at a vineyard listening to wine buffs will do that to you. Between you and me, I was fidgeting with boredom by the end. If anyone offers me a job doing vineyard excursions, remind me to say no.'

'People like James are useful, though. Neither Pedro nor I know very much about wine, so we relied on a woman called Isabella to suggest the right ones for us to stock.'

'Maybe we should introduce her to James if things don't work out between him and Abby.' I laugh.

'She's married, and she wouldn't thank him for the flowers. She once threw a man out of one of her wine tastings because he was wearing aftershave.'

'Why?'

'She said the scent of the aftershave would interfere with his ability to smell the wine properly, and therefore it was a total waste of her time him being there.'

'Wow. How to win friends and influence people. I doubt he bothered to darken her doorstep again.'

'You'd think so, wouldn't you. But he was back for the very

next tasting, minus the aftershave of course, and now they're married.'

'Goodness.'

'Exactly. And do you know the one thing he has never, ever done?'

'Wear aftershave?'

'That, and he's never bought her flowers. Her nose is a sensitive instrument, so they don't have any distracting odours in the house.'

'That's a bit extreme. Anyway, Abby works in construction so I don't think she's going to have the same sensitivity.'

'Ha. Building sites are no place for a woman,' Rosa declares, shrugging her shoulders expressively.

'Nonsense, Rosa. This is the twenty-first century; I think we've left those kinds of attitudes behind.'

'I can't help being traditional.'

* * *

The smell in my room is intoxicating when I go to collect the flowers just before dinner, and I pause for a moment, breathing in the heady scent. I like a glass of wine as much as the next person, but I'd happily smell this over all the stuff James was discussing with the people at the bodega. The guests are all enjoying their pre-dinner drinks on the terrace, so I take a circuitous route to place the flowers in the bucket by James' chair. The bouquet really is enormous, and I need both hands to carry it. One thing is for certain – Abby is not going to be in any doubt how James feels about her. I just hope she lets him down gently if she decides she's not interested.

The decanter with the wine is already waiting, so James has obviously been here before me. I carefully place the bouquet into the bucket, but it takes a few goes before I feel confident enough to let it go without the bucket tipping over. We're going to have to split it across several vases once he's delivered his grand gesture.

I normally steer well clear of the control room unless I have a specific reason to go in there, but Gus has asked Rosa to serve the date-night tables tonight so I can watch, given how much effort I've invested in James and Abby today. Chris and Tim are in front of their enormous monitors, which are showing live feeds from every camera. Gus, Dom and Raquel are standing behind, watching and occasionally requesting a particular feed be made full screen so they can see it more clearly.

'Ah, here's our matchmaker,' Gus comments with a smile. 'There aren't any spare headphones I'm afraid, so you'll have to lipread if you want to know what they're saying.'

'It's OK. I reckon I'll be able to pick up what I need to from their body language.'

The table is currently vacant, but James and Abby appear after a few minutes. He's very solicitous, I notice, holding her chair for her while she sits down and helping to push it in. The conversation appears a little stilted, which is hopefully just down to James's nerves.

'Give her the flowers,' I mutter under my breath.

'Patience,' Gus laughs.

I watch as he pours a glass of wine from the decanter for each of them and wait for him to start swirling it around and sniffing it like he did this afternoon. This could be make or break; if he goes into wine-bore mode, he'll lose her at the first hurdle. To my astonishment, however, he merely chinks his glass against hers and they each take a sip. I see her eyes widen as the liquid hits her mouth and, from her expression, I think she's being complimentary about it. A few sentences pass between them before he reaches down and lifts the bouquet out of the bucket.

If Abby liked the wine, I think it's safe to say the bouquet has blown her away. She's beaming as she takes it from him and sticks her nose in for a good sniff.

'Oh, he won't like that,' I murmur.

'Why?' Gus asks.

'It'll upset all her olfactory nerves and probably ruin the taste of the wine.'

'I didn't know you were a connoisseur.'

'Oh, I'm not. It's just something Rosa said.'

Gus looks perplexed but obviously decides not to delve any further into Rosa's and my supposed wine knowledge. On screen, Abby has carefully laid the bouquet on the grass, got up from her seat and planted a smacker of a kiss on James' cheek. He looks as if all his Christmases have come at once. From that point on, everything seems to go swimmingly. The conversation appears to be flowing naturally, and they demolish the wine between them. At the end of the meal, Abby picks up the flowers but, like me, needs two hands to hold them. To my delight, James offers to carry them for her, cradling them in the crook of his arm as they stroll hand in hand back towards the terrace and the rest of the group.

'I'd better go and take those off him,' I say to Gus. 'Rosa's waiting with some vases so we can split them up and put them in her room.'

As if on cue, James appears with the flowers just as I exit the control room.

'Happy?' I ask him.

'Ecstatic. It couldn't have gone better.'

'I was expecting you to do the swirling and sniffing thing with the wine. I'm glad you didn't.'

'Of course I didn't!' He looks amused. 'That kind of thing is fine when you're tasting a wine, and I did check it when I was decanting it, but not when you're drinking it. Anyway, she really liked it, and that's the main point. Can you do the necessary with these?'

'Of course,' I tell him. 'Give them to me.'

As I climb into bed and close my eyes later that evening, the lingering scent of the flowers is still clearly discernible, but that's not what comes into my head as I start to drift off to sleep. Normally, I think about Jock, but tonight he's joined by images of a beautiful, derelict hotel in Margate.

19

It's Saturday morning, and I'm up early for an airport run to get the first batch of guests to catch their flight home. The audience vote on last night's live final was close, but Flo and Rob just beat Abby and James to the top spot. The two couples have very sweetly agreed to split the winnings between them, although I think the main prize as far as Flo is concerned will be the inevitable swell in the number of her followers. Abby and James don't appear to be disappointed and have made all the right noises about trying to take their new relationship back into the real world, although I'm not sure how that's going to work with him being in London and her in Leeds.

The London-bound contestants, including James, Flo and Rob, are busily piling their luggage into the boot of the minibus as I walk out of the house. Indoors, Chris and Tim have already started the laborious task of dismantling all the cameras under the watchful eye of Rosa.

'Do you mind if I sit up at the front with you?' James asks as the other guests climb into the back of the bus.

'Not at all,' I tell him. I get the impression he wants to chat, so

I'm a little surprised that he doesn't speak until we're out on the main road.

'I just wanted to say thank you again for everything that you did,' he murmurs, obviously not wanting the people in the back to overhear.

'All part of the job, and I'm glad things worked out so well for you. I hope you and Abby will be happy together.'

'Mm.'

'What?'

'I'll confess that I'm worried she'll get home, come to her senses and promptly dump me.'

'Have more faith in yourself, and in her. You two have been inseparable since your date night. Why would she suddenly want to dump you?'

'It's been a bit of a bubble, being in here. She didn't have work to distract her, well, apart from that brief thing with the hotel. When she gets home and real life hits, things will be very different...' He tails off.

'You're worried she might be *Too Busy for Love*?' I ask.

He obviously recognises my deliberate pun because he gives a weak smile. 'Something like that. Her life is pretty full on, flitting between her sites in Kent and head office in Leeds, and I do quite a lot of travel with my work as well. When are we going to find time to see each other?'

'You have to find a way to make time. It doesn't matter how busy you are, you always have time for things that are important to you. Do you have to be in London for your job?'

'No. Most of my work is over the phone, so I can pretty much do it from anywhere, as long as there's internet access and a phone signal.'

'There you are then. There's no reason why you can't work around her schedule. Lots of couples face these kinds of challenges very successfully. I don't see why you shouldn't be one of them.'

He doesn't look convinced and stares morosely out of the windscreen until we're on the outskirts of Palma, when his phone pings with a message.

'It's Abby,' he tells me excitedly when he's read it. 'She wants to know if I'm free next weekend.'

'Are you?'

'I am now.'

* * *

Having dropped a considerably happier James and the rest of the group at the airport, the irony of my advice comes home to roost as I drive back to the villa. Jock and I were in a bubble much like the contestants on the show but, unlike them, we never gave ourselves the chance to take it into the real world. Although we're back to exchanging the occasional text message, he's still taking up way more headspace than a normal friend would. I know it's irrational to miss him and think about him this much, as he's evidently settled into his new job in Glasgow and I still feel my ultimate goal is to find another position in London once I've pushed Hotel Dufour far enough down my CV. There's literally no point dwelling on him, as I've told myself firmly several times without success. I need to focus on work; Casterbridge Media are very pleased with me and anxious to work with me again, according to Gus, but that hasn't translated into a solid offer yet.

Now that Villa Madrigal is nearly empty again, there isn't going to be much for me to do apart from helping Rosa to give all the rooms a thorough clean and act as translator while the production team dismantle their stuff. The house seems weirdly lifeless after the hustle and bustle of the show, and I'm amused to see that even Rosa looks a little lost.

'I won't deny that it's been stressful,' she tells me when I ask her about it. 'But it's also been a lot of fun.'

'You must have other guests booked in, though?'

'Yes, but this house, it needs to be full to truly bring it alive. The next guests are a couple from America with their two children. They come every year and I like them, even though we can only talk using Google translate on the computer.' She sighs. 'It's going to be a bit dull compared to this, though.'

'What are you two talking about?' Gus asks as he strolls in, making Rosa bristle. I've told him several times how territorial Rosa is about her kitchen, but he never takes any notice.

'Rosa's just saying how much she's going to miss us,' I tell him.

'Then you can share the good news if you like. HQ are absolutely delighted with the series and have commissioned another one for next year. I've just got off the phone with Mr Mancini's PA and we have verbally agreed to come back here to film it, so that's something for us all to look forward to. I hope you'll come again, Beatrice.'

'If I'm free, I'd love to,' I tell him before breaking the news in Spanish to a cautiously pleased Rosa. 'Now, if nobody needs me for a bit, I thought I might go for a swim. The pool has been calling me for weeks.'

'Go. Enjoy,' Gus says with a smile. 'You've earned it. We'll probably come and join you later.'

As I power through the deliciously cool water, my mind turns to my own departure in a couple of days' time. I've contemplated phoning the agency several times, but I've really enjoyed myself here and another Casterbridge job would show prospective employers that they rated me. It's a gamble: if Casterbridge come

through then I've won. If not then Ludlow beckons while the
agency look for something else, and that's a definite lose. After a
few more lengths, a third option starts to crystallise. If I can find
somewhere other than my parents' hotel to hide out in, that
would allow me to let Casterbridge go to the wire. If they haven't
offered me anything by the time I leave, I could potentially call
the agency on Monday, and then it becomes a straight race
between them. Gus has promised me a glowing reference either
way, so I've got something other than Hotel Dufour to show
prospective employers.

My first thought was to head up to Glasgow to see Jock.
However, I read and re-read our text exchanges and, although
he's interested in what I'm doing, there's not the slightest hint
that he might be missing me, so I ruled it out in the end. Even if
Jock does feel the same, it doesn't solve all the other issues about
long-distance relationships. If I'm sure of anything, it's that my
future glittering career is unlikely to be waiting for me in Glasgow. What I need is somewhere not too expensive, preferably
within easy reach of London, to spend a week or two while I line
up the next job.

By the time I've finished my swim, I reckon I've come up with
just the place. After drying myself off, I head to my room, fish out
my laptop and begin the search for Airbnbs in Margate. It's not a
part of England I've ever visited, but it's obviously a reasonably
popular destination if the number of properties that appear is
anything to go by. An hour later, having checked that there is a
direct train service to London, I've booked myself in to a one-
bedroom flat within walking distance of the station. Abby's hotel
is still sharing space with Jock in my dreams, and I'm determined
to see it in the flesh before she lets it crumble to dust. I know it's
fanciful but I've dreamed about it almost every night since she
showed me the pictures. The dreams either start in the lobby,

which has been restored to its former glory, or at the railway station. The station is heavily romanticised, with enormous locomotives hissing clouds of steam and platforms full of bell boys helping the first-class passengers unload their trunks, wheeling them on trolleys out to the waiting taxicabs as seagulls swoop overhead, filling the skies with their haunting cries.

The hotel is ablaze with lights as we approach, and the curved glass either side of the front door sparkles as the headlights sweep across it. In the lobby, the centrepiece is a gorgeous dark mahogany reception counter with geometric golden patterns on the front and rows of heavy keys on ornate keyrings hanging behind it. The eras do muddle themselves up a bit here; modern touches such as a computer and telephone switchboard somehow occupy the same space as elegant ladies, dripping with jewellery and wrapped in the kind of fur stoles that were incredibly popular in the 1920s but would be severely frowned upon today. They're smoking cigarettes in long holders and their free hands are casually draped on the sleeves of the gentlemen with them, who are wearing white bow ties under starched wing collars, with white waistcoats and dark tails. Everyone is sipping champagne from delicate coupe glasses. From the lobby, my mind's eye follows the guests into the large ornate dining room, where a string quartet is playing classical music that's barely audible over the hum of chatter and the clink of silver cutlery on bone china. Once again, the eras muddle as staff hurry in and out of the modern stainless-steel kitchen, bringing beautifully presented plates of food to the appreciative diners. The kitchen itself is presided over by none other than Jock, of course, resplendent in his immaculate and crisply starched chef's whites, with a tall chef's hat completing the look.

It's at this point that the dream turns sour. The first hint of trouble comes when a scream goes up from the guests as the dining room wall begins to collapse, revealing an enormous digger with Abby at the controls. She's impervious to their cries as she scoops them up, tables and all, into the bucket of the digger before swinging it round and dumping them unceremoniously on a rubbish pile. The digger roars furiously, black smoke belching from its exhaust as she punches hole after hole in the wall, leaving a trail of smashed furniture, musical instruments and rubble in her wake. This is the scene that usually wakes me up in a cold sweat.

I know the dream is pure fantasy; everything Abby told James and me by the pool makes total sense. If there was any chance of the building surviving as a hotel, it would have done so. And yet, for some reason, I can't let it fade into obscurity without at least visiting to pay my respects. Is it wrong to believe that buildings have a soul? Something within them that carries traces of their history? I watched a programme on TV ages ago about place memories and how they might trigger some people to see ghosts, and it resonated with me. Every hotel I've worked in, including Hotel Dufour, has had its own unique personality that extends beyond the people working and staying there.

So I'll make the pilgrimage to bid this beautiful old lady goodbye while I'm sorting out my next job. I know it's irrational, but I don't have anything else to do and its certainly more appealing than spending any time in Ludlow.

20

My pilgrimage is not off to a promising start, as Margate station couldn't be further from the romantic vision in my dream if it tried. The weather isn't helping, to be fair. After weeks of warm Mallorcan sunshine, the UK has decided to welcome me home in typical style, with grey skies, drizzle and a surprisingly chilly breeze coming off the sea. The station is largely deserted; a couple of mangy-looking seagulls are fighting over the remains of a packet of crisps that someone has left on a bench and, further up the platform, a teenage boy in a hoodie is trying to impress his female companion by performing stunts on his skateboard. If the bored expression on the girl's face is anything to go by, it's not working.

As I follow the directions on my phone, my case bumping along behind me on the uneven pavement, my impressions of Margate don't really improve. It feels shabby in that way that only a British seaside resort can manage, and I'm starting to agree with James's dismissive assessment that it's a dump as I follow the instructions to release the key to my lodgings from the key box on the wall of a dilapidated-looking terraced townhouse. Thankfully, things improve dramatically once I get inside my flat, which is airy and nicely decorated. The owners have evidently decided on a nautical theme, as there are seaside trinkets dotted around the place, but it's just the right side of tacky. The rooms are generously proportioned, with high ceilings adding to the feeling of space. Part of the living room has been partitioned off to make the small galley kitchen, but it's still big enough to comfortably house a big squishy leather sofa, coffee table and wall-mounted TV, plus a small dining table with two chairs. The bedroom is dominated by a king-size bed, but I'm pleased to see there's also a wardrobe and chest of drawers. The bathroom is a little dark and poky as there's no window in there, but it's perfectly adequate for my needs.

Having unpacked and made a shopping list, I decide to take another look at the town that's going to be my home for the next week or two. It's a strange mix. It doesn't take me long to find the main beach, and I'm amused to see a few hardy souls swimming in the sea, despite the weather. The beach itself is wide and sandy, with a road separating it from the amusement arcades, fish and chip restaurants and souvenir shops that are practically compulsory in this type of place. At the eastern end of the beach sits the Turner art gallery, but what I find more interesting is the range of shops and restaurants I encounter as I continue past it and walk further into the town. There's a definite bohemian feel as I explore; at one point, I stare in bewilderment at a tiny restaurant. The menu is inviting and I'm tempted to book a table until I notice that it only opens one day a week, in the evening. How anyone can make a successful business with a model like that is beyond my comprehension, but it's evidently possible in Margate. In London, and everywhere else I've been in the UK, the rents are so high that businesses will open seven days a week for as many hours as they're permitted to make the most of every drop of potential revenue but, as I walk the streets of Margate, I discover that they're much more casual about things like that here. Some of the shops that should be open have signs on them saying things like *Back at 4.30* or even, in one case, *Back on Wednesday*.

I've decided to delay my visit to Abby's hotel until tomorrow, when the weather forecast is for sunshine so, after stocking up on food and essentials, I head back to the flat to unpack it all and spend the rest of the day exploring. The more I unearth, the more fascinated I am. Down one street, I find an unassuming entrance to something called the Shell Grotto. Curious to find out more, I buy a ticket and go down the stairs, only to find myself in the most incredible set of rooms and passageways, all covered from floor to ceiling with seashells. The guidebook informs me that there are over four million of them in here, but nobody knows who built it or what for. After a happy half hour exploring the subterranean chambers, it's disconcerting to climb the staircase again and find myself back on the same very ordinary street.

By the time I've had a wander around the Turner Contemporary, Margate's charms are definitely starting to make an impression on me and I'm in good spirits as I head back to the flat. My phone pings with a message, and I'm very surprised to see that it's from my mother.

> What is the plan now the show has finished? Are you still in Mallorca/coming home/doing something else?

I type out a swift reply while I'm cooking my evening meal:

> I'm currently in Margate.

Her response is immediate.

> What's in Margate?

I consider how to answer that question for a while. I'm obviously not going to tell them that I've come on a bizarre quest to visit a derelict building that's been haunting my dreams while also avoiding them. They'll only convince themselves I'm having some kind of breakdown, not that I suspect they'd do very much even if I was. In the end, I type:

> It's a surprisingly interesting place, actually. Love to you both xx

No reply comes. Their interest in the world outside Ludlow has always been limited, so I'm not surprised. As I dish up my simple supper of pasta carbonara and salad, it occurs to me that this is the first meal I've had to cook for myself since before I started at Hotel Dufour. Rosa and Jock would probably find lots of things wrong with it, but I'm rather pleased with myself. I pour a glass of wine from the bottle of inexpensive Merlot that James wouldn't approve of either and settle down in front of a quiz show on the TV. After I've had a look at the hotel tomorrow, I'll update my CV and have a chat with the agency. Gus is certain that Casterbridge Media will be in touch very soon, but I can't afford to wait around for them any more.

* * *

When I open the curtains the next morning, I'm pleased to see the weather is exactly as forecast. Although the ground is still wet and there are puddles galore, the sky is bright blue with only the occasional fluffy white cloud. However, there's still a brisk breeze coming off the sea, so I wrap my coat around me before heading out in search of Abby's hotel. This time, I'm heading west, away from the town centre, but I've only been walking for a quarter of an hour or so before I spot the unmistakeable profile of the building I'm looking for.

Although Abby's pictures gave the impression that the hotel was well situated, the reality is even better. Directly in front of the hotel is a road that rather grandly calls itself the Royal Esplanade, but in front of that there is nothing but grass, then the beach and sea. It's a stunning vista. Unfortunately, the building itself, when I get closer, is looking decidedly squalid. The ground-floor windows have been boarded up and the local graffiti artists have taken full advantage of this new canvas for their work. Weeds are poking up abundantly through the broken concrete at the front, and the gorgeous curved glass and magnificent front door are barely visible through the thick steel meshed security gates that have been bolted over them. Some of the upper windows, which haven't been boarded up, are already broken, and tattered curtains are flapping in the breeze behind them. If water is getting inside, which it must be doing, it will only hasten the demise of the building, and, for a moment, I wonder whether the broken windows were Abby's doing to help nature along. I don't think she's the type of person who would do that though. I hope not, anyway.

As I walk round to the side, there is another heavy steel mesh gate blocking access to what must be the car park. I press my face up against it but all I can see is more broken tarmac with weeds poking through, some abandoned plastic crates that would have had beer bottles in them once, and the remains of a sign with the logo of the budget hotel chain on it.

I retrace my steps to the front of the building and cross the road so I can get a better view of it as a whole. Despite the peeling white paint and graffiti, it's still easy to see the beauty underneath.

'Tragic, isn't it?' a voice says next to me, making me jump. I turn to find myself face to face with a man who must be ninety if he's a day. 'I spent some of the happiest years of my life here, and now look at it,' he continues. 'Are you from the development company?'

'Umm, not exactly,' I tell him. How to explain who I am without sounding like a lunatic? 'A friend told me about it, and I'm into art deco, so I wanted to come and have a look.'

'It used to be the most marvellous place.' The man sighs. 'But times change, don't they? We're in tune, The Mermaid and me. She was at her best when I was in my prime, and now we're both old and worn out.'

'The Mermaid?'

'That's what it was called. You can still see the name at the top if you look carefully. The last lot never bothered to remove the sign, just stuck the board with their logo over it.'

I look up, and he's right. At the very top of the building is a large slab, into which the words *Mermaid Hotel* have been carved.

'There was the most beautiful mosaic of a mermaid in the lobby,' the man continues, lost in his thoughts. 'We were trained never to walk across it, but always around the edge. Different days, eh?'

'You worked here?'

'Oh yes. I started as a pot washer when I left school and worked my way up to doorman. I even met my wife here; she was a housekeeper.'

'I'm trying to picture what it must have looked like back then.'

'Oh, she was beautiful.'

'Are you talking about your wife or The Mermaid?'

'Both,' he says wistfully. 'We had our wedding reception here.

Happiest day of my life. Every time I walk past, I can see my Annie in her dress, even after all these years. Of course, we could never have afforded it normally, but it was hotel policy to offer employees a free reception if they wanted it.'

'Wow.' I'm trying to picture him as a young man with his bride but I'm struggling. 'I don't mean to sound pushy,' I say after a moment, 'and please feel free to say no, but I don't suppose you have any photos from back then, do you?'

'Lots.' He laughs. 'I'd be happy to show them to you if you have time. I'm Reginald, by the way.'

'Beatrice.'

'What a lovely name. Delighted to meet you, Beatrice. I live in the retirement home a little further up if you're happy to follow me and don't mind listening to the nostalgic ramblings of an old man.'

'I'd love that. Thank you.'

When Reginald said 'a little further up', he really meant it. His retirement home is almost next door to The Mermaid so, despite his slow shuffle, supported heavily by his walking frame, it only takes us a couple of minutes to reach it.

'If the warden asks, you're my great-niece,' he tells me conspiratorially as he holds his pass up to the holder next to the front door. 'They mean well, but they can be a little over-protective.'

The heat when we get inside is almost stifling, but I follow him past the front desk and down a long corridor with doors on either side.

'This is me,' he says, holding his pass against a door lock on the left, which beeps and clicks open. I follow him in and find myself in a bright, airy room with a bed on one side and a sitting area on the other.

'Take off your coat and make yourself comfortable,' Reginald says, indicating an overstuffed sofa. 'I never sit there any more. I can get in it, but then I have to get someone to help me out. I sit there, in my whizzy chair.' He points to a very ordinary-looking armchair by the window. 'Would you like a cup of tea or anything?'

'I don't want to put you to any trouble.' Although he's abandoned the frame now he's indoors, he's still terribly frail and I can see he has a tremor in his hands. Making tea would be a big effort for him.

'It's no trouble.' He laughs. 'I just phone the kitchen and someone brings it.'

'In that case, tea would be lovely, thank you.'

He places the order, adding chocolate digestives for good measure, and then crosses to a glass display cabinet, which has various ornaments in the top half, and drawers underneath.

'I'm awfully sorry,' he says. 'The albums are in the bottom drawer, but I can't get down there. Would you mind?'

'Not at all. Tell me what I'm looking for.' I bend down, open the drawer and, after I've moved a few things out of the way, Reginald instructs me to bring out a large leatherbound book. It's heavy and a little unwieldy, but I've soon freed it and laid it on the sofa. Reginald lowers himself carefully into his 'whizzy' chair and closes his eyes. For a moment, I'm worried he's gone to sleep, but then he says, 'Open it. I know every picture in there like the back of my hand.'

The first picture is of a young woman in a simple white dress, smiling shyly at the camera.

'That's my Annie,' he says without opening his eyes. 'January the fifteenth, 1953. I was twenty and she was seventeen. We were married for sixty blissful years before she passed away. Cancer.'

'She's beautiful,' I tell him sincerely.

'She was. Turn the page,' he instructs.

By the time the tea and biscuits arrive, we're about halfway through and I'm fizzing with excitement. I'm currently looking at a shot of Reginald and Annie getting out of the car at the front door of the hotel. The curved glass is sparkling, and the mosaic of the mermaid is clearly visible inside.

'The next picture is the dining room, with our wedding cake set up at the end. Rationing hadn't ended yet, so the whole family sacrificed their coupons so we had enough butter, sugar and eggs to make it.'

I turn the page and study the picture. Obviously, the dining room doesn't match the one I saw in my dreams; that would just be weird and creepy. It is opulent, though; there are large multi-paned mirrors around the walls, typical of the art deco style, and even though the photos are small, faded and black-and-white, I can tell the table linen is thick and good quality.

A thought comes to me. 'Reginald?' I ask.

'Yes?'

'You don't have to tell me, but I gather the current owners planned to turn The Mermaid into flats but were prevented because of local objections. Do you know anything about that?'

He laughs softly. 'I wouldn't read too much into that if I were you. I think people were happy enough as it's a bit of an eyesore at the moment, but the rumour on the grapevine is that Dennis Mountford, a local councillor, wanted to buy it and develop it himself. When he was outbid, he countered by getting the planning application blocked, even though it was exactly what he'd planned to do. I think he's hoping the developers will lose interest and sell the building to him for a knock-down price.'

By the time we get to the end of the book, Reginald is obviously tired, so I make my excuses and leave. He's very kindly let me photograph some of the pictures on my phone, and I promise to call by and see him again soon. I'm relieved to get out of the oppressive heat into the fresh air but, as I walk past The Mermaid again, I stop and gaze up at its lifeless, blank windows. Now that I've seen what it used to be like, there's no way I can let it just crumble.

'I can't promise I'll succeed,' I tell it suddenly. 'But I'm going to try my very best to save you.'

21

I feel energised as I make my way back to my rented flat. I know that my initial response after seeing the building and talking to Reginald was purely emotional. I'm also perfectly aware that emotional responses are not good ways of making business decisions but, if anyone can make a case for reopening The Mermaid as a hotel, it has to be me, surely?

When I get in, instead of updating my CV as I'd intended, I start to make a list of the things I need to put into a potential business plan. The first thing to do is check out the competition and come up with a unique offering that's going to both fit in with Margate's bohemian vibe but also stand out from everything else on the market. Getting an idea of the costs to restore the building is beyond me at the moment, but if I can come up with a strong enough concept to tempt Abby, maybe she'll buy into it and help with that side of things.

It's late by the time I get to bed, but this time, my recurring dream about the hotel and Jock is not interrupted by Abby with her bulldozer, which I take as encouragement.

The next morning, I present myself at the library the moment it opens and, with the help of the librarian, start searching their digitised archives for any information about The Mermaid. There isn't much. I find an article from 1929 about its opening, but the picture is very poor quality and I can't decipher much from it. Reginald's pictures are much better from that point of view. There are a couple of articles from the Second World War period, when it was used as a temporary soup kitchen and dormitory during the evacuation of Dunkirk, but then nothing until two recent articles. The first confirms that it had been purchased by the BudgetWise Hotel chain, and the second is a mere paragraph stating that it will not be reopening.

Feeling uninspired by the building's history as a way to make it stand out and succeed, I turn my attention to the competition. This proves much more fruitful. What I discover is that there are loads of privately run bed and breakfast type establishments, but there's only really one hotel that caters to the market that I think I would want to chase. When I check their online bookings, it shows me no availability for the next three months. That in itself doesn't mean much – they could be closing for maintenance or something – so I decide to call them and pretend I'm looking for a room for a special anniversary. The receptionist is friendly but explains to me that they're usually booked months in advance and it's worth planning further ahead next time.

This is all I need to know to tell me that not only is there a market for the type of hotel I'd want The Mermaid to be but, crucially, the demand is currently outstripping capacity, which means there's untapped potential. Now all I need is something to differentiate The Mermaid from the competition. I open the notebook I've bought to keep all my jottings and thoughts in, turning the pages until I have two blank ones in front of me. I write the words *Come for...* at the top of the left-hand page and *Stay for...* at the top of the right. I need a unique selling point to draw customers to us rather than anywhere else, and a reason to make them want to choose Margate over anywhere else for a holiday.

The *Stay for...* column starts to fill quite quickly, as Margate has a lot to recommend it once you scratch beneath the surface. The *Come for...* column has just one entry so far but, if I can pull this off, it could be very good for me as well as The Mermaid.

* * *

By the end of the week, I've collated as much as I can and typed it all up into a proposal to put to Abby. I've spent several hours talking with Reginald and getting a feel for how The Mermaid was in his day, not because I want to recreate it exactly as it was, but to capture the spirit of it. My notebook is full of jottings: the ones I like emphasised as I've traced over the words repeatedly, but others crossed out as impractical or ludicrously expensive. My mouth is dry and my heart is pumping as I dial the number I found for Abby's firm on their website.

'Atkinson Construction, Donna speaking. How may I help?' Like Abby's, the voice has a broad northern accent.

'Hi, I was wondering if it would be possible to speak to Abby.'

'She's not in the office at the moment.' Her tone is brusque. 'Can I take a message?'

'My name's Beatrice,' I explain. 'I met her on the set of *Too Busy for Love* and—'

I don't get any further because Donna cuts me off and her tone of voice changes completely. 'I'm so sorry. I thought you were a cold caller. I meant what I said about Abby not being in the office, but I'm sure she'd love to hear from you. Would you like her mobile number?'

'Please.'

She reels off the number and I dial it as soon as we disconnect.

'Abby Atkinson.' She sounds distracted.

'Hi, Abby. This is Beatrice, from *Too Busy for Love*. Is this a bad time?'

'Beatrice!' Her voice is warm. 'Of course not. How are you?'

'I'm well, thank you. I'm actually in Margate at the moment.'

'Really? What are you doing there?'

I need to play this very carefully. 'I had some free time and I've never been here before, so I thought, why not? I passed your building on one of my walks.'

She sighs. 'Is it too much to hope that it's fallen down?'

'Not yet, but I did have an idea for something you could do with it, if you're interested.'

'I'm certainly interested if it'll get my dad off my back. He's still going on about it, would you believe. I'm currently hiding out at one of our sites in Ashford under the pretext of carrying out an extended inventory check.'

I can't believe my luck. 'Do you think you'd be able to take time out from your inventory check to come and visit Margate? I'm sure there must be things you need to look at here.'

'Let me check my calendar. I've got meetings tomorrow morning but I could probably clear my diary after lunch. It's only fair to warn you that I think I've covered all the possibilities where that building is concerned, but it would be nice to see you anyway. Are you going to give me any clues about what you've come up with?'

'Sorry,' I reply. 'It's strictly show and tell. It'll be worth your while, I promise.' Of course, there's no way I can predict how she's going to react to my plan and I am a little disheartened by her initial caution, but I have nothing to lose. If she doesn't go for it, I can walk away knowing I did my best.

'Fine,' she says. 'I'll drop by after my meetings. I'm not completely sure what time I'm going to finish, so shall I call you when I'm ten minutes away from the building?'

'Perfect,' I tell her.

When the call disconnects, I'm feeling elated but also nervous. I spend the rest of the evening going over and over my notes, looking for holes or things I haven't considered.

By the time I go to bed, I'm as confident in my plan as I can be. Now all I have to do is sell it to Abby.

* * *

The weather is on my side at least, I think as I stride towards the building the next day to meet Abby. The sun is out and the chilly breeze has decided to give it a rest, so it's actually quite warm. As I approach the building, I spot her climbing out of a sleek silver Porsche parked across the road. She looks very different on her home turf; her chestnut hair is tied back and she's wearing faded jeans and a loose shirt.

'Hi, Beatrice,' she says when I reach her, pulling me into a hug. 'It's nice to see you again.'

'And you. Dare I ask how things went with James after you got back?'

She smiles. 'We're taking it slowly, but the signs are good. He's in Birmingham at the moment, some wine fair at the NEC, but I'm taking him home to meet Dad at the weekend.'

'So you're going to try the long-distance thing then?' I ask carefully. If she and James have unearthed some magic ingredient, I'd like to hear it in case there's something that could help in my situation.

'We haven't figured that part out yet,' she replies breezily. 'All I'm hoping is that grilling James will give Dad something else to focus on besides his daughter's misguided redevelopment idea. Thinking of which, tell me what you've got planned for this building of mine.'

'I will, but can I ask you a favour first? Can I have a look inside?'

'If you like. You'll need appropriate clothing though.'

'What kind of appropriate clothing?' I glance down at my jeans and trainers, which I thought were quite practical.

Abby looks me up and down. 'I always carry a spare hard hat and hi-vis jacket, so you can borrow those, but ideally you'd have a proper pair of boots on too.'

'Oh, sorry. I didn't know.'

'Not to worry. I think we can make an exception this time; just be very careful and look where you're going.' She pops the bonnet of the Porsche and fishes out two hats and vests, giving one of each to me. She also pulls out a very scruffy-looking pair of boots, which she slides her dainty feet into after removing her ballet pumps. Then she leans into the cabin and fishes out a bag that seems to be full to the brim with keys. She rootles through for a while, before selecting a bunch attached to a tag with *Margate* written on it in marker pen. Finally, she extracts a torch from the glovebox.

My breath catches in my throat as Abby unlocks the padlock on the steel mesh gate at the front, which swings open with a metallic squeal. This is the first time I've seen the front door and the glass panels on either side properly and, despite the fact that they're filthy, they still look amazing. I peer in to see if I can spot even the faintest hint of the mosaic, but the lobby floor is now carpeted. Abby unlocks the front door and holds it open for me to step through.

The smell inside is exactly as you'd expect in a building that has been disused for a while. It's an unpleasant mixture of damp and something acrid that I can't quite identify.

'Rats,' Abby remarks matter-of-factly as I wrinkle my nose. 'Be careful where you tread.'

It's very dark in here but, even before Abby flicks on the torch, I can tell that all the period features have long gone. The thin, cheap carpet underfoot is threadbare, the exquisite mouldings on the walls are nowhere to be seen, and ugly doors have been installed where the staircase used to be. It's poky and uninviting; nothing like the sumptuous reception area that I saw in Reginald's photos.

The dining room is also depressing. Cheap plastic chairs are stacked upside down on flimsy collapsible tables. There's a kind of buffet area on one side, with a serving hatch. My trainers stick to the lino floor as we cross it to peer through the hatch into the kitchen. There's very little equipment in here; everything of value was patently sold off either when the budget chain bought the hotel or when it sold up. There are two large fryers, a stove and a dilapidated oven against one wall, with a sink and commercial dishwasher against the other.

'Seen enough?' Abby asks.

'Is it safe to go upstairs?'

'Yes. The building is actually very sound, structurally. I thought that was a plus when I bought it, but I'm coming to regret it now.'

We make our way back into the lobby, and Abby pushes open one of the doors to reveal not the sweeping staircase of Reginald's photos, but a concrete one with steel banisters. It's obviously been installed to save space and make room for the lift, but I can't help feeling sad about it. I follow Abby up, being careful where I put my feet, until we reach a corridor.

'Take your pick,' she tells me, gesturing at the row of doors. I know which room I want to see, but it takes me a minute to get my bearings and figure out which door probably belongs to it.

'That one,' I say to Abby. We walk carefully to the end of the corridor and she pushes open the door.

The room is as tragic as everything else I've seen, and the curtain is still fluttering in the breeze from the broken window, but none of that matters. The view from here is magical, and I sigh with pleasure.

'Are you going to tell me what this is all about?' Abby asks after a minute or so.

'Yes. Let's go somewhere a bit more conducive and have a cup of tea.'

As I follow her downstairs and out of the front door, waiting for her to lock the steel gate securely behind her, I mentally start gearing myself up for the sales pitch of my life.

22

'OK,' I say to Abby once we're ensconced in the tea room I scouted out for this meeting during one of my walks. 'Before we start, I've made some assumptions. The first is that you want the quickest return on your investment based on the lowest outlay.'

'Not quite the lowest outlay,' she corrects. 'We're not a "pile 'em high, sell 'em cheap" construction firm. Our customers expect quality.'

'But you still want the best return on your investment, right?'

'Absolutely.'

'So if I were to tell you that my idea could get you a much higher rate per square foot than yours, for a lower initial outlay, what would you say?'

'I'd say bring it on. What's the idea?'

'Reopen it as a hotel.'

Her face falls. 'Beatrice—' she begins.

'Hang on. Hear me out,' I interrupt. 'You're going to tell me that it's not viable as a hotel because it wasn't viable before. You're probably also going to tell me that you're not in the business of hotels. Am I right?'

She sighs. 'Yes, on both counts.'

'But this is where I come in. Because I *am* in the business of hotels, and I'm confident that there is a market that we can tap into. Let's say, for the sake of argument, that the council has a sudden change of heart and approves your planning application. As well as the repairs and redecoration, you're going to have to make some fairly big changes to the interior layout. I imagine that's expensive.'

'It's not cheap, but cheaper than starting from scratch.'

'Fair point. But if you leave it as a hotel, you don't have to make those expensive changes. You just have to bring it back up to standard. Now, which do you think makes more money per square foot per night. An apartment or a hotel room?'

'It's not as simple as that, from our perspective. I'm sure a hotel room is more profitable on a rental basis, but we're not planning to rent out these apartments. We sell them and walk away. The cash goes into our next development.'

'Let me put it a different way then. At the moment, the council is not going to let you do anything with the building, so your cash is tied up until it either falls down or they change their minds. We're not talking about pocket money here. I'm giving you the opportunity to press ahead with a plan that they can't turn down, and start getting your money back out in a much shorter time frame.'

She bites into her carrot cake and chews thoughtfully, taking a sip of tea to wash it down. I'm desperate to tell her all the other good things about my plan, but I force myself to stay silent. She needs a moment to absorb what she's heard so far. Given that she's no longer openly shooting me down, I must have made some impact.

'What makes you think it's viable as a hotel?' she asks eventually. 'If a big company like BudgetWise couldn't make it work, that's a red flag, don't you think?'

'They had the wrong model,' I tell her simply. 'They were catering to the lower end of the market and there are already lots of players in that area who've been here for much longer than them. Also, Margate just isn't a chain hotel sort of place. People who come here want to immerse themselves in its unique culture, and a chain hotel doesn't fit with that at all. What people want is boutique. That's what The Mermaid was when it was successful, and that's what it should be now.'

'The Mermaid?'

'That's what it was called. There's still a slab with the name at the top of the building. Here, let me show you something.' I spread out some of the pictures I've printed off from my shots of Reginald's wedding album on the table. Once again, I let silence fall as she studies them.

'Where did you get these?' she asks as she leafs through them.

'I met a guy who used to be the doorman there. It was hotel policy to provide a wedding reception free of charge to any members of staff who got married.'

'What a lovely idea. It looks so different, doesn't it. So...' She tails off.

'Glamorous?' I offer.

'That's it. It's almost impossible to believe it's the same building.'

'But it is. Apart from whatever they've done to the staircase, it's structurally identical. It just needs its mojo back.'

'You have no idea how much I wish that were true, but it's more complicated than that.' Abby's face is no longer wreathed in nostalgia. Business Abby is back in the room and I can sense she's losing interest. 'You can't just recreate, when was this?'

'1953.'

'Exactly. You can't just recreate 1953 and expect it to work now because it did then.'

'I'm not suggesting that. We need a thoroughly modern USP, but I think I have it.'

'Go on.'

'Point one. Don't relaunch as a budget hotel. Go for the top end of the market.'

'I'm not sure Margate is a "top end of the market" kind of town.'

'I disagree. There's currently one four-star hotel here and I checked; it's fully booked months in advance.'

'Which shows that the market is already catered for. Surely that would be the same mistake as launching a budget brand. We'd just be outclassed by the competition.'

'I don't think we would, but that's not the point. The point is that the advance bookings for the other hotel show us that there's untapped demand for a quality product. Demand we could take advantage of.'

'How?'

'That comes back to the USP,' I tell her, relieved that I've managed to get her back on the hook. I collect up the photos and spread out the come for/stay for list that I've typed out.

'Come for the food?' She sounds doubtful.

'Yes. Food is a big theme here in Margate, along with art and some of the other things I've listed in the "stay for" column. What we need is an exceptional offering from a talented chef to tempt the foodie market.'

'Do you have someone specific in mind?'

'As a matter of fact, I do.'

'It's not Rosa from the show, is it? I mean, her food is good but I don't imagine she'd react well to the British climate.'

'It's not her. It's a guy I worked with at my previous job.'

'Where's he working now?'

'He's at a restaurant in Glasgow at the moment.'

'Hmm. When someone says "foodie destination", Glasgow is hardly the first place to trip off the tongue.'

'He's good, I promise.'

'I see. And he's on board with this plan, is he?'

'I haven't mentioned it to him, actually.'

'Why not? If he's the kingpin of your business plan, the whole thing kind of goes up in smoke if he says no, doesn't it?'

'Yes, but equally it wouldn't really have been fair to get his hopes up if you were going to turn me down flat.'

She takes another bite of her carrot cake, and I can practically hear her brain whirring as she chews.

'How much longer are you planning to stay in Margate?' she asks eventually.

'I've booked the apartment for another week. I was supposed to be applying for jobs this week but I've been a bit busy with this, so I've pushed my other plans back.'

'Let's just say, and this is absolutely theoretical, that I went for this. It's going to take a while to get the building up to standard. What are you going to do while the building works are going on?'

'I'd want to be onsite,' I tell her firmly. 'I have a vision for this building, so I'd want to be very hands-on.'

She looks wary. 'When you say "vision"...'

'You can't take a building like that and just turn it into a bland corporate hotel, with identikit rooms all painted the same colour. It needs personality and period features. It needs the right fittings, the right furniture. Not repro crap; the punters will spot that immediately.'

'Sounds expensive.'

'Not necessarily. I mean, there will be some areas where we

have to spend a bit of money, but you can pick up period decorations from auctions and stuff. It'll still come in at a fraction of the cost of converting it to flats, I reckon.'

'Do you have project management experience?'

'No,' I admit.

'But the role you've just described to me, being onsite and supervising the renovations, that's project management. I'd have to be mad to give you that level of responsibility when you don't have any experience.'

'I may not have project management experience but, as I told you, I *know* this industry. I know what works and what doesn't. If you bring in someone who knows how to manage a project but doesn't share the vision, you'll end up with something soulless.'

Abby drains her tea before picking her phone out of her bag and dialling a number.

'Ella, it's me,' she says into the handset. 'What's your diary looking like tomorrow?'

She frowns as she listens to the answer. 'Fine. Can you reschedule that and come to the Margate site instead? Bring Noah and John too. Oh, and can you pick up a pair of boots for me please? Size...' She looks at me expectantly.

'Five,' I tell her.

'Size five,' she repeats into the phone. 'Yes, there's a plan, but I want your input to see if it's viable or not. Great. I'll see you here at ten.'

She disconnects the call and fixes her eyes on mine. I'm sure she's at least a year younger than me, but she's exuding the kind of authority you'd normally see in someone much older.

'I'm not promising anything,' she says firmly. 'But I'm prepared to look into this a little further. Ella is my senior project manager in the south of England. She knows her stuff and I trust her implicitly. Noah is her fiancé and also one of my site

managers – there's almost nothing he doesn't know about buildings – and John will never forgive me if I don't let him come too.
We'll see you onsite at ten tomorrow. Don't be late.'

With that, she gathers her belongings together and strides
out of the café in the direction of her car, leaving me open
mouthed.

23

After Abby left, my first thought was to rush over and tell Reginald, but sense won out in the end. It wouldn't be fair to get his hopes up when all I'd managed to do was secure another meeting with more people who would probably be against my idea. I did visit him, but we confined our conversation to chatting about his daughter, Jeannie, who lives in New York with her husband. He's prodigiously proud of her, showing me pictures not only of her and her husband, but their children, children's spouses and grandchildren. They used to fly him and Annie over once a year, but that stopped when she fell ill and now Reginald feels he's too frail to make the journey. They talk frequently on the phone, and she's coming over to see him in a month or two.

I've elected not to say anything to Jock just yet either. In my fantasies, he jumps at the chance, comes down and we pick up exactly where we left off, but I'm realistic enough to know that he may not feel like that at all. The messages we've exchanged have been friendly, but no more than that, so it's possible he's moved on. If he has, that will definitely be a dent in my dream, but I've realised it doesn't diminish my enthusiasm for the hotel project, so I've decided to hold off until I have a concrete proposal to put to him.

It's just before ten and I'm making my way to the hotel to meet Abby and the others. I'm scanning the parked cars for her silver Porsche, but there's no sign of it. I'm just about to congratulate myself on getting here first when she climbs out of the passenger side of a van. A large, bearded man who looks to be in his fifties steps down from the driver's seat. Behind this van I spot another, and a woman and man who are probably my age get out of it. I'm guessing the woman is Ella; she's blonde and very pretty. That would presumably mean the dark-haired man with her is Noah, so the big guy with Abby must be John. After brief introductions during which I learn that Ella is also from Leeds but John and Noah are both local, Ella hands me a large box with a pair of sturdy-looking boots inside.

'Put those on,' she instructs. 'They'll feel like lead weights at first, but they'll protect your feet and you'll soon get used to them.' I glance at her and notice that she's wearing a similar pair under her jeans, although hers are scuffed from hard use.

She's not wrong. I feel like I've got clown's feet once I've put them on, but there's no time to get used to them as, after handing me the same hi-vis jacket and hard hat I wore yesterday, Abby crosses the road and unlocks the steel mesh gate.

'Fuck me, Abs!' John exclaims, looking around him in dismay once we've congregated in the lobby. 'Couldn't you find a proper shithole to buy?'

'You're funny,' she tells him sarcastically. 'You should be on the stage.'

'So what's the plan?'

'The original plan was to redevelop it as flats, but the local council didn't like that. So then I was just going to mothball it until it either fell down or the council changed their mind, but Beatrice seems to think it could be viable to reopen as a hotel.'

'What do you want from us?' Ella asks.

'I'd like you to take a look around and try to get a feel for the amount of work that might be needed to bring it up to standard. I'm not talking super detailed at this stage, just t-shirt size it.'

'What, like small, medium, large and fuck-off enormous?' John continues, still staring around him in disbelief. 'I think we can answer that one right now.'

My heart sinks. In my down moments, this is what I feared would happen. They're going to tell Abby it'll cost a fortune and she'll promptly lose interest.

'When you say "up to standard", what are we talking about?' Noah asks.

'I want to open it as a four-star hotel,' I tell him. 'That's what it was in its heyday. In the public areas like here and the dining room, I want to restore the art deco feel. I'd also like to rip out that hideous concrete staircase and recreate the original. Here, I've got a picture of what it looked like.' I fish out the photos and go through them until I find the one of Reginald and Annie that clearly shows the sweeping staircase in the background, handing it to Noah.

'You've got no chance of that, darlin',' John observes dismissively, looking at the picture over Noah's shoulder. The way he's just called me 'darlin'' gets my back up and I decide I don't like him.

'Why not?' I demand, trying and failing to keep my tone calm.

'Fire regs,' he says simply. 'You would probably have got away with it as an original feature of a historic building, but a new one would have to conform to all the latest regulations, including fire doors and stuff. That's probably why they took it out in the first place. Am I right or am I right, Michael?'

'He's right, I'm afraid,' Noah agrees, completely ignoring the fact that John just called him by the wrong name. 'There might be something else we can do, though. Is there a service staircase as well as this one?' he asks Abby.

'Yes, at the rear of the building.'

'OK.'

'What are you thinking?' Ella prompts after a pause.

'I agree with Beatrice. If you're going to recreate the art deco vibe in here, you can't do it with those hideous doors and a concrete staircase. But, instead of trying to recreate the original staircase, we could put in some retro-style lifts here. You know, the ones they used to have back in the day with dials above the doors and arrows pointing to which floor they're at. There's a company that makes them. All the lifting gear and so on is modern, but they look antique. As long as the service staircase meets the fire escape requirements, I think we'd be fine.'

'What about the floor?' I ask, pointing at the geometric-patterned tiles in the photo. 'Can we recreate that at least?'

John walks over to a corner of the room and lifts the carpet, which comes away easily to reveal a sheet of wood underneath. 'We might not have to,' he remarks. 'Who wants to bet that they just laid this over the top of it to take the carpet? Give us a hand, Michael.'

'Why does he keep calling Noah Michael?' I ask Ella as the two men set to work trying to lift the sheet of wood and Abby wanders over to watch.

'It's his thing.' She smiles. 'Everyone has a nickname, the more obscure the better. Noah is named after Michael Fish.'

'Who's he?'

'A weather forecaster who was famous for failing to predict a hurricane in 1987. Noah predicted the flood in the Bible, Michael failed to predict the wind. See?'

'Blimey, that is obscure. Have you got one?'

'Yes. I'm Carol, after Carol Vorderman. She was the math-
ematician on the TV program *Countdown* back in the day. I'm the
project manager, so we're both, to use his words, "numbers
birds".'

'What about Abby?'

'She doesn't get one because she's family.'

'They're related?'

'No, but he's been like a surrogate father to her. She lived with
him and his wife for a while when she first came south to work
on site, and she still stays with them whenever she's down. It was
John that persuaded her to apply for your show.'

'Really?'

'Yup. He was worried Abby was working too hard and not
playing enough. Don't be fooled by him. Underneath the gruff
exterior lies a real teddy bear.'

'I can hear you, you know,' John calls from the corner of the
room.

'You were meant to,' she replies with a smile.

'Gotcha, you bastard,' John exclaims triumphantly as he and
Noah lift a large sheet of wood off the floor. 'Oho. Come and have
a look at this.'

It's absolutely filthy, but underneath the piece of wood that
John and Noah are now leaning against the wall is a clearly
recognisable pattern.

'Assuming they're not too damaged, they'll probably clean up
pretty easily,' Noah observes. 'I wonder why they covered
them up?'

'All BudgetWise hotels have to have the same look and feel,'
I explain. 'Grey carpet with the company logo in the public
areas, dark blue in the bedrooms. You might not be able to tell
which town you're in, but you'll always know you're in a

BudgetWise hotel. I did a case study on them when I was at university.'

John is evidently not at all interested in the BudgetWise business model, as he's now examining the light switch, flicking it on and off a couple of times.

'Power's off,' Abby tells him.

'I figured. The wiring looks modern though, so we might not have to replace it. Another big win. What's through here?'

We follow him into the dining room and the three of them spend a moment taking it in.

'Vision?' Ella asks.

I show her the picture of the room set out for the wedding.

'Those mirrors are gorgeous,' she remarks. 'I wonder where they are now?'

'Flogged off, I expect,' John replies.

'They won't be cheap to replace,' Ella observes, still staring at the picture.

'I don't know,' Noah says, taking the picture off Ella and carrying it over to the window for a better look. 'I reckon we could knock something together that would look the part, even if it wasn't genuine.'

'What about furniture, though?' Ella persists. 'If you're going for art deco as the room vibe, modern furniture is going to clash. Either that or you're going to have to track down someone who can make it in the same style, and bespoke is always pricy.'

She's got a point and my mood slumps again.

'Can I suggest something controversial?' Noah says suddenly. 'What if you didn't go art deco in here?'

'What do you mean?' I ask.

'What kind of food are you planning on serving?'

'If I get the chef I want, it'll be modern British, showcasing local, seasonal ingredients. Why?'

'That's what I thought. If you restore this room to its art deco days, you're kind of creating an expectation that the food will also reflect the period. Do you see what I'm saying?'

'But if we don't, it will clash with the rest of the hotel,' I point out.

'That's not always a bad thing. Hang on a minute. There's a hotel my brother-in-law took my sister to for their wedding anniversary last year. Let me see if I can find it.' He fishes out his phone and, after a minute or two of searching, shows me a website. The hotel is exactly what I had in mind when I described my dream to Jock all those weeks ago. It's a stone country house with mullioned windows set in beautiful gardens. He scrolls through some of the photos, showing me wood panelled sitting rooms with huge fireplaces and gorgeous bedrooms with sumptuous ensuites.

'What's your point?' Abby asks after a moment.

'What I'm showing you is a historic building with all its period features, right?'

'Yeah.'

'Now look at the dining room.' He flicks to a picture showing an incredible modern room, with glass walls opening onto the garden.

'Oh wow. That's stunning,' I breathe.

'Yes and, according to my sister, it actually fits with the vibe of the place perfectly.'

'So what you're saying is modern food needs a modern room?'

'I think so, yes. It also solves a lot of problems.'

'OK,' I say after reflecting for a moment. 'I suggest we pause this room until we have the chef on board, but in principle, I like the idea if we can do it well.'

'Let's have a look at the rest of the place then,' John declares, leading the way back into the lobby.

It takes us a couple of hours to tour the whole hotel, as Ella, John and Noah want to look in every room and discuss the plans for it. In the end, we agree that the standard rooms will have a common look and feel, but the larger rooms with the sea views will be where we focus on creating something a bit more special to attract a premium price. What I'm most happy about, however, is that most of the issues with the building appear to be cosmetic rather than structural, and the others are talking about it as if it's a feasible project now. Even John has stopped harrumphing and started writing notes on his pad.

'Right,' Abby says as she locks up a while later. 'Next steps. Ella, I want you to work with Noah and John to put together a report on what we'd need to do to the building. Beatrice, you need to write me a full business proposal with projected costs and revenues. If we're really going to do this, we've got to put a bullet-proof case to my dad. Oh, and you'd better talk to your chef. If we don't have him on board, we won't have a USP.'

She's gone for it and given me an excuse to talk to Jock. I could dance for joy.

24

As soon as I get back to the flat, I send a message to Jock.

> I have news...

He's obviously at work as he doesn't reply until late afternoon.

> Sounds intriguing. Go on.

I smile as I type:

> Can I call?

> Sure.

You know how it feels when you've been in a dark wood, and you step out into the sunshine and automatically turn your face to soak up the warmth? Seeing Jock on my screen is like that. Although we've texted, this is the first time we've actually talked since leaving Hotel Dufour.

'How's Margate?' he asks.

'Interesting. I mean, the first impressions aren't great, but once you start to scratch under the surface, it's got a lot going for it.'

'How long are you planning to stay?' I've told him about visiting Abby's hotel, but not my plan to save it, so this is a reasonable question.

'I'm not sure,' I tell him with a smile. 'I might hang around. Something's come up, actually.'

'Don't tell me, let me guess. You've fallen in love with this derelict hotel and you're conjuring up a plan to reopen it.'

'How did you know that?' I ask in amazement.

'It's obvious. What do you need from me?'

'Why should I want anything from you, apart from to talk to you?'

'Because I know you. If all you wanted was to tell me about your plan, you'd have done it in a message. You're calling because you want something.'

'You make me sound like an awful person!' I exclaim.

'Sorry, I don't mean it like that. Let me rephrase it. You're calling because you want to ask me something, rather than just give me information.'

'I prefer that,' I tell him, feeling mollified.

'So what can I do for you?'

'How attached are you to Gregory's?' I ask.

He grins. 'I'm always open to offers.'

'Look. I can't promise anything, but I'm putting together a business plan to sell to Abby and her father, and I'm going in hard on food being the USP. I'm thinking of you for that.'

'Sounds interesting.'

'That's what I hoped you'd say. We need to be realistic though, Jock. If this comes off, it could be amazing, but I'm trying not to get my hopes up too high, and I don't want to get yours up either. There's a long way to go, but if you're interested enough to do me a sample menu to include in the pitch, that would be brilliant.'

'Leave it with me,' he replies. 'When do you need it by?'

'As soon as possible, really. I think Abby is planning to go up to see her dad in a few days.'

'I'll get something to you tomorrow.'

* * *

What I hadn't realised was that Abby was expecting me to come with her to pitch the idea to her father. After a hair-raising journey north in her Porsche, followed by an overnight stay in the local BudgetWise hotel, the irony of which was not lost on me, we're now pulling up outside Abby's family home, which evidently also serves as the head office of Atkinson Construction if the brass plaque on the gatepost is anything to go by. I've been frantically reading online articles with titles such as *The Ten Secrets of Sales Success* and *Seven Ways to Pitch Perfection*, and I've honed my presentation to within an inch of its life, but I'm still nervous. Abby's driving yesterday didn't help, as she weaved through the traffic, using the power of her car to slide into seemingly impossible gaps on the motorway and perform overtaking manoeuvres that had my heart in my mouth more than once. I'm very glad that, whatever happens, I'll be travelling back on the train later. If I were a cat, the journey up here would have used at least six of my nine lives.

Abby enters a code on the keypad next to the large, ornate, wrought-iron gates and they swing open silently, allowing the car to crunch across the deep gravel of the driveway, where an expensive-looking SUV is already parked.

'I haven't said anything to Dad about your plan,' Abby explains as she turns off the ignition. 'I want him to come into it totally fresh, OK?'

'OK.'

The front door opens before we reach it, and the resemblance between Abby and her father is strong enough to leave me in no doubt as to the identity of the man standing on the threshold.

'Dad, this is Beatrice,' Abby tells him. 'Beatrice, this is my dad, Christopher Atkinson.'

'Pleased to meet you,' he says to me warmly, holding out his hand. 'Abby's being very secretive, but I gather you have a plan to put right her rather expensive mistake.'

Abby rolls her eyes theatrically. I suspect this is a well-worn theme.

'Come on in,' Christopher continues, seemingly oblivious to his daughter's irritation. 'I'll put a fresh pot of coffee on, and then you can tell me all about it.'

By the time we settle down in the office, my initial nerves have given way to my enthusiasm for the project, and I feel sharp and confident as I take Christopher through my presentation. I quickly discover that, underneath the genial exterior, he's as astute as his daughter when he's talking business. There have been several areas where he's stopped me, asking either for more detail or clarification. I've taken him through the projected costs and revenue in forensic detail, and he's grilled Abby on some of the other points, mainly around the work needed to restore The Mermaid.

'I have to admit it's a good plan,' he says eventually. 'You clearly know your stuff, Beatrice, and you've done your home-work. It's impressive.'

Mentally, I'm crossing my fingers and I suspect Abby is doing the same.

'There's just one problem,' he says after a long pause.

'What?' Abby asks. 'Do you need to go through the projections again?'

'No. There's nothing wrong with any of what you two have said. Your presentation is very compelling and, although there are a couple of things I'd do differently, I honestly can't see any major holes in it. In the right hands, I have no doubt that you would be successful. But the fact is that I'm not the right hands. We're a construction company, not a hospitality company. To put it bluntly, I don't know anything about hotels and it's not an industry Atkinson Construction has any intention of entering.'

I don't know what to say. I stare dumbly at the presentation as my dream crumbles to dust in my head. Next to me, Abby is staring at her father with a curious expression on her face. The atmosphere in the room is tense and uncomfortable and I suddenly feel the need to be as far away from here as possible.

'I understand,' I murmur as I hastily gather the presentation documents together and get to my feet. 'Thank you for your time, Christopher. Abby, I wish you the best of luck with the building.'

'I'll give you a lift to the station,' Abby offers, not taking her eyes off her father.

'It's OK. I'll get a taxi.'

'Nonsense.' She gets swiftly to her feet. As she opens the door into the hallway, she turns back to her father. 'I'm just going to run Beatrice to the station,' she tells him, 'and then we'll have a chat. OK?'

'My mind is made up, Abby,' he replies.

'I'm sure it is. That doesn't mean there isn't anything to talk about, though, does it?'

Once again, their eyes lock and I get the impression an entire silent conversation is playing out between them. I'm no longer interested, as I'm mainly focused on keeping my composure while I bid goodbye to Christopher. Abby is silent as she drives me, but I can practically hear her mind whirling. Knowing her, she's already working out her next plan, but I no longer care. With just a few words, my bid to save The Mermaid is over. As the train pulls out of the station, I send Jock a message.

> The pitch didn't work. Sorry.

His reply comes instantly, and I read it through my tears of frustration.

> Ah well. You tried.

25

'You seem a little subdued today. Is everything all right?' Reginald asks gently. We're having tea in his small living room on the day after my disastrous meeting with Abby's father; I'm sitting on the sofa as usual and he's in his 'whizzy' chair, which I now know earned its name because it has a motor inside that lifts it up when he presses a button and makes it easier for him to stand.

'Sorry,' I reply. 'The truth is that I've been working hard on a project for the last couple of weeks, but it's all come to nothing and I'm disappointed.'

'Of course you are,' he says sympathetically. 'What was the project?'

'I was working with the owner of The Mermaid,' I tell him. 'I thought we could restore it to its glory days and reopen it.'

'What a lovely idea. What happened?'

'The owner's father.' I sigh deeply.

'Oh. Perhaps you'd better start at the beginning.'

'It's not a very interesting story.'

'I'm sure it is, and I don't have anything else to do. Humour an old man.'

'Fine. So you know the council turned down the planning permission to turn it into flats—'

'Dennis Mountford and his cronies,' Reginald interrupts disapprovingly.

'Exactly. But I know hotels, and I reckoned there was a good business case to reopen it.'

'BudgetWise evidently didn't think so, but they ruined the place anyway. Go on.'

'I've done a lot of research, and there's room in the market for a four-star hotel with a superb restaurant.'

'People round here certainly like good food,' he agrees.

'I even found the perfect chef. Well, I didn't exactly find him. I've worked with him before, and I knew he'd be just the right person for a place like this. I crunched all the numbers and they looked pretty good, so I honestly thought it was in the bag.'

'So how did the owner's father wreck it?'

'They're partners in the business, so she needed his consent to go ahead and he didn't give it. It's not his fault – I understand where he's coming from – but I'm just frustrated that such a promising idea got shot down purely because he doesn't understand the hotel industry and doesn't want to learn.'

'Oh dear. What happens now?'

'I start job hunting. I put it off while I was working on the Mermaid plan, but I realise now that it was just a stupid fantasy and I need to focus on getting my career back on track.'

'Will you stay here in Margate?'

'I don't think I can. Sorry.'

'That's a shame, but I understand. I'll miss chatting to you, though. You've brought a lot of happiness to this old man while you've been here.'

'I'll miss you too,' I tell him sincerely.

'Will you make me a promise?' he asks, and I notice his eyes are a little moist.

'You have to tell me what it is first,' I reply carefully. I'm very fond of Reginald, but I'm not going to commit to anything just because he wants me to.

He leans forward in his chair and takes my hands in his. His grip is surprisingly strong as he fixes his eyes on mine.

'Live well,' he says earnestly. 'Love wholeheartedly. Die happy. Those are the only things that matter. If you do the first two, the third is guaranteed. With the right person beside you, you come to realise that everything else is just white noise. That's what my Annie and I had, and that's what I want for you.'

I sigh. 'You make it sound so easy.'

'Oh, it's not. It's hard and it's often painful. But you have to focus on what matters. Look at me; I'm a decrepit old man who can barely walk and I think we can both agree that the best years of my life are far behind me. But my heart is full and I'm happy. Why? Because I've given and received love in abundance throughout my life. I know you're focused on your career, Beatrice, but don't forget to love. Promise me?'

'I'm not sure I'm very lucky where love is concerned,' I tell him as he releases his grip.

'What makes you say that?'

I tell him about my week with Jock and my plan to recruit him as the chef at The Mermaid. If he's surprised by my involvement with Hotel Dufour, he hides it well and listens sympathetically. When I'm finished, there's another long silence before he speaks.

'You could go to be with him in Scotland.'

'I could,' I say quietly. 'But I'm scared. What if he doesn't feel the same way? He was friendly on the call, but no more.'

'If he's prepared to uproot from Glasgow and move down here to be with you, it doesn't sound like he was just being friendly to me.'

I laugh in spite of myself. 'When did you get so wise?'

'Oh, I don't know that I'm wise, particularly. I'm just old and I've seen a lot of things. Shall I tell you something interesting about old age? The older you get, the less you understand the world because it moves on so fast, but the more certain you feel about your opinions. If you don't believe me, come and have tea in the communal sitting room one afternoon. Sometimes I think actual fighting is going to break out.'

He smiles and, as I look at him, I can feel the love emanating from him, not just for me but for his fellow residents. I just wish I could have given him something back.

'I'm genuinely sorry about the hotel, Reginald,' I tell him quietly after a minute or two.

'Don't be. It was a nice idea to try to save it, but another of the many lessons I've learned over the years is to hold tightly to people but lightly to things. Yes, it would have been lovely to see it restored, but someone is bound to do something with it one day. Land in this country is too expensive just to leave it sitting around doing nothing for ever. Even if they do something absolutely frightful to it, I'll probably be dead by the time it happens, so I'm not going to waste what little time I have left worrying about it. I'm more worried about you. What does your gut tell you to do about the boyfriend?'

'My gut agrees with you, that I should go and see him, but my head isn't so sure.'

'If you don't mind me hijacking a phrase from your generation, he sounds like a keeper. What's the problem?'

'I'm afraid of making a fool of myself. What if I've misread the signals and he's moved on?'

'It's a risk, but what's the worst that can happen? You go up there and things don't pan out? Then you dust yourself off and make a new choice. But if you don't go up there – if you let him go – a part of you will always wonder if you made the wrong decision.'

'You're right.' I sigh. 'I let him go once, and it was definitely the wrong decision.'

'Exactly.' He smiles. 'And it's like the old saying goes—'

'Reginald,' I interrupt. 'If you're about to come out with some cliché like "it's better to have loved and lost than never to have loved at all", please don't. You were doing so well.'

His frail frame shakes with laughter. 'That's exactly what I was going to say. It may be a cliché, but there's wisdom in it. Think about it, will you?'

'I will,' I promise him.

Reginald is right, I realise as I walk back to my flat. I'd be a fool not to go to Scotland and at least talk to Jock some more. Quite apart from the fact that I'd kick myself for letting him go a second time, it's not like I have anywhere else I urgently need to be. I can afford to leave it another week before contacting the agency.

My thoughts are interrupted by the sound of my phone ringing in my bag. I fish it out, hoping that it will be Casterbridge wanting to offer me another job, but the caller ID tells me it's Abby. It sounds selfish, but I don't really want to talk to her right now. I'm sure she's only calling to apologise for the way the Mermaid project turned out, and I don't want to be dragged back into all of that now that I'm starting to think about my next steps. I stare at it until the voicemail kicks in and then put it back in my bag. By the time I get back to the flat, however, she's called twice more and I'm unpleasantly surprised to find her waiting for me on the doorstep.

'Hello, Abby.'

'Where have you been?' she accuses, completely failing to pick up on the lack of enthusiasm in my greeting. 'I've been calling you.'

'Oh, umm, sorry. My phone must be on silent.'

The lie is no sooner out of my mouth than my phone pings loudly in my bag to remind me I have voice messages. Abby raises her eyebrows.

'Fine,' I admit. 'I've been avoiding your calls.'

'What? Why?' She looks genuinely hurt.

'Look, Abby,' I say with a sigh. 'I know you mean well, but it's done. I don't need to pick over the bones of the Mermaid project. It got shot down and, although I'm disappointed, I'll live. You don't need to come and check up on me.'

'Oh, for goodness' sake,' she says crossly. 'I'm not checking up on you. Hurry up and let me in. We need to talk.'

I gaze at her. Her eyes are unusually bright and she seems even more revved up than usual. I open the door and guide her into the flat, where she perches on the sofa, drumming her fingers impatiently on her thighs while I put the kettle on for a cup of tea.

'Are you all right, Abby?' I ask her carefully. 'You're acting a little weird.'

'I'm fine. I'm merely excited and trying to share some brilliant news with the one person I thought would be as excited as me, but you seem strangely uninterested in hearing it.'

Oh shit. I've called this completely wrong and I feel like a terrible person suddenly. This must be to do with the show and James, rather than the hotel. I sit down next to her and wrap her in a hug.

'Oh, Abby, congratulations!' I exclaim. 'When did he pop the question?'

She stares at me like I've grown an extra head.

'You think James proposed?' she says slowly. 'We've only just started going out. Why would he propose?'

'Some people just know, don't they?' I reply lamely.

'Let me set you straight. Contrary to popular opinion' – she gives me the side-eye – 'I'm not engaged. I'm here about The Mermaid. There are a couple of adjustments I need you to agree to but, assuming you're happy, we can start work more or less straight away.'

'But your father clearly said that he wasn't going to go into the hotel business.'

'No,' she corrects me. 'He said that Atkinson *Construction* wasn't going to go into the hotel business. But that doesn't mean that Atkinson *Hotels* can't.'

26

'I'm not following you,' I tell Abby as she stares at me, her eyes sparkling. 'He was very clear about it. He said he didn't know anything about hotels and it wasn't an industry he had any intention of entering.'

'And he won't be. Atkinson Hotels is my company. Well, it will be, once I file all the paperwork and stuff.'

'I think you'd better start from the beginning,' I say carefully.

'Fine. After you left, Dad and I had a long chat. I knew he was up to something, because why bother grilling us on all the business plan and stuff if he had no intention of following through? Basically, there were three points he made. One, that the business plan was good and the best chance of getting a return on The Mermaid – congratulations, Beatrice. Two, that he didn't want his core business to be distracted or put at risk by a venture he didn't understand. Three, that there was one part of the model that he felt I needed to revisit – I'll come on to that in a minute. So, the upshot is we set up a new subsidiary company with me as sole director. Atkinson Construction transfers ownership of The Mermaid to Atkinson Hotels, which refurbishes it and reopens it.

There will need to be appropriate governance and repayment clauses, obviously, but that's the general gist.'

'Why a subsidiary company?' I ask. 'Surely the risks are the same.'

'No. As long as Dad stays firmly out of the picture and Atkinson Hotels is seen to be operating completely independently of the main company, they're immune from liability if the hotel company goes belly up. It's a way of protecting the main business. Dad will still advise me, us, informally if we ask for it, but he'll have to be very much in the background.'

'So that's it? We're good to go?' It sounds too good to be true.

'Nearly. I mentioned that there was something that Dad picked up on and, on reflection, I agree with him. It concerns the food.'

'Go on.'

'We both feel that we need a name people recognise in the kitchen. I'm sure your guy is good and everything, but he's an unknown.'

My mind is whirling. Jock was a big part of my plan.

'What if I could get him to come down? Give you and your dad a chance to try his food?'

'Sorry,' she says. 'We need a name. If we're going to get a return on our investment, we need the punters lining up from day one. We simply don't have time to wait for your guy to establish a reputation from nothing. It's a done deal, Beatrice. If you can't work with it, tell me now and walk away.'

I sit in silence for a moment. I do want The Mermaid more than I could have imagined, but Reginald's words are playing in my mind. If I accept this condition, I'm basically kissing goodbye to any chance of a future with Jock. I need to see if I can get her to come round. After all, if Christopher isn't in the driving seat, he shouldn't get to choose the chef, should he?

'Did you have someone specific in mind?' I ask.

'Yes. Emilio Marcuso. Do you know him?'

'I know of him, yes. But he's got restaurants all over the country, hasn't he? How much time will he actually spend in the kitchen of The Mermaid? If you're going to sell a celebrity chef, the customers need to see him, otherwise they'll think it's just a cynical marketing ploy.'

'They don't seem to feel like that in his other restaurants. From what I can tell, they're all extremely successful. Why shouldn't that translate here?'

'Because... because that's not the Margate vibe, Abby! This place is all about authenticity.'

'There are chain restaurants here. I saw several on the sea front.'

'Yes, but—'

'But nothing. What's your guy's name?'

'Andrew. Andrew McLaughlin.'

'Right. Surely you can see that "Marcuso at The Mermaid" is going to be a much bigger draw than "Some guy called McLaughlin that you've never heard of at The Mermaid". Emilio puts us on the map from day one, Beatrice. If we're going to have a hope in hell of this project succeeding, we need that. This isn't open for negotiation.'

I sigh. I still think she's wrong, but it is her business and I need to decide if this is a hill I'm going to die on. I try to weigh up the options rationally. If I take her up, then I have a guaranteed job back in the hotel industry. No more fixed-term contracts, and maybe I can use the fact that she's overruled me on the chef as leverage to get my way in other areas. But I lose Jock. On the other hand, I could turn her down but, not only does that feel like biting the hand that's trying to feed me from a career perspective, I still might lose Jock. If I were in a cartoon, I'd have a mini Reginald on one shoulder urging me to live well and love wholeheartedly because the rest is just white noise. On the other would be rational Beatrice, telling me that I've invested too much in my career so far to let a man, even a man like Jock, derail me.

'I don't get it.' My thoughts are interrupted by Abby. 'This is a tiny adjustment to an otherwise brilliant plan. Are you seriously telling me you're prepared to throw the whole thing in the bin over it? You're the one who dragged me over and sold me the whole idea of reopening as a hotel. It was your blinder of a pitch to my father that convinced him it was viable. I'm offering you what you want on a plate and now you don't want it any more? What the actual, Beatrice?'

And, with that, I know what I have to do.

'You're right,' I tell her as mini Reginald disappears in a puff of smoke and I kiss goodbye to any hope of reconciliation with Jock. 'I'm going to stick my neck out and say I still think Emilio isn't the right choice for Margate, but it's a comparatively small change to the plan and I'm sure he knows how to make these things work. So yes. I'm in.'

'Thank the Lord for that,' she breathes. 'The whole project would have been dead in the water without you. Right. Next steps. We need to get Emilio on board.'

'You mean you haven't *spoken* to him?' I ask, appalled. 'You gave me the impression it was done and dusted.'

'Of course I haven't spoken to him. There wouldn't have been anything to talk about without you, and Dad and I only agreed to go ahead yesterday afternoon. I'm good, but not that good.'

She pulls her phone out of her bag and dials a number. 'Hi, Donna. It's me. Beatrice is on board, so can you see if you can get us a meeting with Emilio Marcuso? Yes, as soon as possible please. Thanks.'

She's smiling as she puts her phone away. 'It can't be as

simple as that,' I tell her. '"Hi, Emilio. I know you're a celebrity chef and everything, but we're opening a boutique hotel in Margate and wondered if you'd drop everything to have a chat with us about it."' I'm allowing myself to hope again. If Emilio says no, maybe I can get Jock on board after all.

She shrugs. 'He's a businessman. It's a business proposition. Besides...' She smiles enigmatically.

'What?'

'He's a member of the same golf club as my dad. They often play together and Dad has his personal mobile number. We didn't just choose him at random, you know.'

I don't know whether to be impressed or dismayed. Choosing a chef based on shared membership of a golf club is hardly good business practice, but I can't deny Emilio Marcuso's reputation. Barely a minute has passed before her phone rings.

'Hi, Donna.'

There's some unintelligible speech before she says, 'Tomorrow? Blimey, that's even quicker than I'd expected. Let me just check with Beatrice.' She puts her hand over her phone and turns to me. 'Emilio can see us at four o'clock tomorrow. He's at Marcuso's on the Strand in London and can spare us an hour between lunchtime and evening service. Will you be ready by then?'

'Ready for what?'

'You need to pitch it to him.'

'What?'

'It's fine. Just use the same pitch you used on Dad. I mean, you might want to adapt it a little bit, obviously. Take whatshis-name out and make it look like Emilio was in the plan from the start. These top chefs can be a bit diva-ish. Can you do it?'

'I don't know. I can try.'

Abby turns her attention back to the phone. 'Donna. Tell

Emilio we'll be there, and can you find me a hotel room in Margate for tonight? Yeah, Beatrice and I need to work on her presentation. Thanks. Oh, and can you email over the contracts for Beatrice to sign as soon as you've finished them? Ta.'

She slips the phone back into her bag and smiles. 'Congratulations and welcome on board, Beatrice. You are officially Atkinson Hotels' first employee.'

Although I'm pleased on a professional level, I feel a little disloyal to Jock by going with Abby's decision without putting up more of a fight, but perhaps it would have been selfish to expect him to relocate down here. After all, all the reasons I shared with Reginald about not moving to Scotland apply to him coming here, and what if our relationship didn't work out? Also, dealing with Abby this afternoon has felt a little like being hit by a runaway train, and I'm conscious that I could plan to use the change of chef as leverage. A thought comes into my mind and, although it's audacious, I decide it's worth a try.

'Abby?' I begin.

'Yes?'

'Here's the thing. You've said to me that this project would be dead in the water without me, right?'

'Yes.'

'So you need me, for this to succeed.'

'Yes. What are you getting at?'

'I just think that maybe I'm bringing more to the table than a mere employee, and that should be reflected in my role.'

Her eyes narrow but, now that I've started, I'm warming to my theme.

'At the start of this meeting,' I continue, 'you said that you were going to be the sole director of Atkinson Hotels. Am I remembering that correctly?'

'It's my family business that owns the hotel, and my family

business that'll be putting up the cash to pay your salary and refurbish it. So yes, I will have the controlling interest.'

'But it's me that's bringing the expertise and the industry knowledge. You might be financing it, but the success of this project depends on me bringing all the different moving parts together.'

'Go on.'

'So, in light of that, I think you should appoint me as co-director of Atkinson Hotels.'

She stares at me for so long without speaking that I start to wonder if I've overplayed my hand. The longer the silence goes on, though, the more convinced I am that this is a concession she needs to make.

'This sounds a bit like blackmail. What happens if I say no?' she asks eventually.

'It's not blackmail. I'm simply asking you to recognise what I bring to the table. It's up to you whether you do that or not. I've said I'm in and I'm a woman of my word. The question is what value you place on me.'

'So you'd do it even if I said no? What's my motivation to say yes?'

'Because it's the right thing to do.'

There's another long silence. I know I've shot myself in the foot by saying I'd work for her anyway. In an ideal world, I'd have thought of this before saying yes in the first place, but these things are always easier in hindsight, aren't they? As I wait for her to make up her mind, I decide that her next move will play a big part in how long I stay. If she says no, it will definitely dent my opinion of her. I'll still get the hotel up and running so it looks good on my CV, but I'll look to move on as soon as I can after that. I like her, but she's shown her ruthless side today, and I don't want to be her doormat.

After what seems like an age, she pulls her phone back out of her bag and dials another number.

'Hi, Dad. Slight change of particulars for the new company. Yeah, I'm appointing Beatrice as co-director. No, it's not up for discussion. This is merely a courtesy call to let you know. Yes, we're meeting Emilio tomorrow. I'll keep you posted. Bye.'

'Any other curve balls you want to throw before we get down to work?' she asks.

I feel vindicated. If I'm going to sacrifice a chance of love on the altar of my career, I need to score a concession to soften the blow, and this is a cracker. 'No, that's it,' I tell her sweetly.

'Right then, partner,' she says and I'm relieved to see she's smiling. 'Let's start putting together this pitch for Emilio.'

27

As the supposedly high-speed train inches closer to London, I can feel my pulse starting to quicken. I haven't visited the capital city since Jock and I went our separate ways back in April, and I'm excited to see it again, even if Margate is now going to be my home. Abby and I were up until nearly midnight last night, putting together the pitch to Emilio, and we had a video call with Christopher this morning to run through it and apply any final tweaks. I'm still very slightly irritated that I've been thrust forward to do the actual pitch again but, as Abby said every time I questioned it, I'm supposed to be the industry expert. Given that I used that to lever my way into a directorship, I guess it probably serves me right.

In my heart, I still don't believe that turning the kitchen of The Mermaid into yet another outpost of Emilio Marcuso's sprawling restaurant empire is the right thing to do. It's not just about Jock; I really feel that we're missing a trick by not having a unique food offering. However, I've been comprehensively outvoted. Although Christopher has no formal involvement in Atkinson Hotels, he made it clear that this was his will, and it was

hard to dig my heels in when he pointed out that Atkinson
Construction would be financing the new company, at least in
the short-term. Abby is also completely certain that a big name
such as Emilio will help to get us off to a flying start. I just hope,
for her sake, that she's right. I also wish I could find the right
words to tell Jock what's happened, but there isn't a nice way to
say he's been pushed aside for a celeb, so I haven't said anything
at all.

I've certainly seen a different side of Abby since I first pitched
the idea of reopening The Mermaid to her. Although she was
pretty outspoken in Mallorca, she seemed a little softer there. In
real life, she's a powerhouse; everything is done at top speed, not
just her driving. Before we left for the station, she'd already set
up a meeting tomorrow with her project manager, Ella, and the
older guy, John. She's also instructed John to crack on with
assembling a team and getting scaffolding erected for the
external works. I'm still not sure about him – I really didn't like
the dismissive way he spoke to me last time we met – but Abby
assures me that he knows his stuff and he'll be worth his (not
inconsiderable) weight in gold. Although Ella will be mainly
remote, as she has a number of sites that she manages, John will
be onsite every day so I'll be working closely with him.

It already seems like an age has passed since I was sitting in
Reginald's sitting room while he urged me to follow my heart and
not be distracted by what he called the 'white noise'. I can't
believe it was only yesterday afternoon. For a moment, I feel a
little guilty about ignoring his advice so quickly, but my feet have
barely touched the ground since I found Abby on my doorstep,
and this will give me a secure future. Surely that's the most
important thing? Maybe, if I can build up The Mermaid and
make it successful, there will be an opportunity later on for Jock
to come down and take on the kitchen under Emilio if he wants

to. After all, he's going to need someone competent to run the kitchen on a day-to-day basis, isn't he? That thought cheers me up no end.

As we leave Ebbsfleet International station behind us, the train finally picks up speed, whisking us past the Dartford Crossing and in towards Central London.

'It's almost like you're driving the train,' I say to Abby with a smile.

'Piss off,' she replies good-naturedly, without raising her eyes from her laptop screen.

* * *

The sun is shining as we hurry out of St Pancras station towards the taxi rank. I try to take a moment to absorb the bustle and hubbub around me, but Abby shoos me into the back of a cab and gives the address to the driver. As he pulls away, her phone rings and her face lights up.

'Hiya,' she says enthusiastically before mouthing the word *James* at me. 'How are you?'

There's a certain amount of banal-sounding chat before she suddenly exclaims, 'Really? But I'm in London too! Yeah, I'm here with Beatrice. We're meeting Emilio Marcuso to pitch him the idea of opening a Marcuso's at the hotel in Margate. What time do you finish? Wait, hang on.'

She turns to me. 'Would you believe that James is in London today as well? I know it's short notice, but would you mind making your way back to Margate on your own after the meeting? I haven't seen him for a couple of weeks. I can catch an early train in the morning so I'm not late for the site meeting.'

'It's fine,' I reassure her. 'Of course you want to see him.'

She flashes me a beaming smile before returning her attention to the phone. 'OK. My meeting should be done and dusted by five. Shall I come to your flat? Great. See you later. Love you.'

'Love you?' I raise my eyebrows. 'That sounds like things have moved on a bit.'

She blushes. 'Didn't your mother ever teach you that it's rude to eavesdrop on other people's conversations?'

'Kind of hard not to when I'm literally sitting next to you.'

'Yes, well. Things are in a good place. We just don't get to see each other often enough. Don't tell Dad, but I'm thinking of moving south permanently. Now that we have a plan for The Mermaid, I've actually got more sites down here than up north so it kind of makes sense. James and I have talked about me moving in with him. Although he does business all over the country, he doesn't spend quite as much time on the road as I seem to, so we might actually be able to have something approaching a normal life. Thinking of which, have you given any thought to your living arrangements?'

'No,' I admit. 'I'll add it to my list of things to do.'

'You could move into the staff accommodation at the hotel if you like. We could ask John to prioritise that. I don't think it needs that much doing to it. A lick of paint, new kitchen and bathroom, and it would be quite habitable, I reckon. Plus, you'd be on site twenty-four seven.'

'It's a nice offer,' I say. 'But there's no heating or hot water, and I don't fancy living on a building site. I'm sure I can find a flat or something until the hotel is properly ready.'

'Suit yourself. We would have rigged up something temporary to give you water and heat, but I can see that the mess might be off-putting. Ah. Here we are.'

As I take in the façade of Marcuso's on the Strand, I have to admit that it does look like an upmarket establishment. The sign is rendered in a minimalist, modern font, as is the menu in a display cabinet attached to the wall next to the door. I cast my eyes over it, which proves to be a mistake as I realise I haven't had time for any lunch in the hustle and bustle of the day so far and I'm actually quite hungry. Having paid the driver, Abby pushes open the door and I follow her inside.

'Abbee!' A short, very rotund, dark-haired man in chef's whites leaps up from one of the tables and rushes over, embracing her enthusiastically.

'Hello, Emilio. How are you?'

'Fantastico!' he enthuses in a strong Italian accent before turning his gaze on me. 'Are you going to introduce me to your friend?'

'This is Beatrice,' Abby replies. 'She's the brains behind the project.'

'I am so excited to hear about it, but first you must eat something.' He claps his hands loudly and shouts in the direction of the kitchen. 'Lorenzo! *Porta un piatto di frutti di mare.* Pronto!'

'*Sì*, Emilio,' a voice calls from somewhere beyond the pass.

'Let us sit, and you can tell me all about this project of yours,' Emilio continues, pulling out chairs for us. 'Unfortunately, I am a busy man, so we have to talk business while we eat. This is not good for the digestion, but...' He waves his hand expressively and sighs, as if this is a cardinal sin. A waiter brings a carafe of water and some glasses, and I start my pitch.

I quickly learn that Emilio is almost as much of a powerhouse as Abby. His attention is laser sharp as I take him through the presentation, and he frequently interrupts to clarify a point or dig further into a proposal. The most enormous plate of lightly battered prawns and calamari appears after a few minutes and, after Emilio has squeezed generous quantities of lemon juice over the top, I take a prawn, sighing with pleasure as I bite into it. It's perfectly cooked and the flavour is wonderful. It's all I can do to stop myself from grabbing the plate and tipping the whole lot into my mouth. Emilio might not have been my first choice, but I can't fault his cooking if this is anything to go by. Although Abby hardly touches the food, Emilio is also digging in enthusiastically, and between us we manage to polish off the entire plateful in a few minutes.

* * *

By the time five o'clock rolls round, we have a verbal agreement. Emilio is unsurprisingly exacting about pretty much every aspect of the business, from the financial model that will see him operating the restaurant essentially as an independent concession within the hotel, to the equipment that will be installed in the kitchen. Even the crockery and glassware have to fit the Marcuso's brand, so his final demand, that his company will take sole responsibility for recruiting and managing all the restaurant staff, wasn't a surprise. In return, we've managed to secure agreement from him that he will be onsite and in the kitchen for the first two weeks to deal with any teething problems and help get the restaurant off to the best start possible.

As soon as the meeting finishes, Abby rushes off to meet James, and I find myself at a bit of a loose end. I don't have any reason to hurry back to Margate, so I decide to take a meandering route back towards the station, which will allow me to soak up some of the buzz of the city before I leave. This quickly proves to be a mistake, as every landmark I pass reminds me forcefully of my week of sightseeing with Jock. Although I'm fairly sure I've made the right move, whatever Reginald says, being back here does fill my heart with a pang of longing for him. At one point, I nearly take a picture of one of the places we visited and send it to him before I realise he'll immediately want to know why I'm in London, and I don't want to have to explain my meeting with Emilio to him. I know it's just business, but it feels like I've been unfaithful to him from a professional point of view.

Without intending it, I realise my route is taking me in the direction of Hotel Dufour and my curiosity kicks in, drawing me towards it like a magnet. When I get there, it's surrounded by wooden hoarding and looks, if anything, even more unloved than The Mermaid. I stand outside for a while, trying to see if it stirs any emotion in me, but there's nothing. When I lift my gaze to the top floor, my heart does quicken, but that's only because I'm remembering Jock and nothing to do with the building. I'm just about to turn away when a door in the hoarding opens and a man in a hard hat comes out.

'Excuse me?' I ask him. 'Are you able to tell me what the plan is for this building?'

He looks at me oddly for a second.

'I used to work here, a long time ago,' I explain. If he knows about Madame's sideline, I hope the 'long time ago' will distance me from her.

'Same as everywhere else,' he says. 'Retail outlets on the ground floor, offices and flats above.'

'Thanks,' I tell him. As I turn away, I realise I couldn't be less interested in the fate of Hotel Dufour. Suddenly, I'm keen to get back to Margate and my new life as soon as possible, and I quicken my pace.

28

We're a month into The Mermaid's transformation and, so far, it's gone relatively smoothly. There was one hiccup, where the council thought we were pressing ahead with the development of the flats and tried to close us down, but that was straightened out fairly easily. With Ella's help, I've learned to navigate the project-planning software she likes, and we speak on the phone at least twice a week. John has also proved to be an unlikely ally. To begin with, I took exception to him calling me 'darlin'' in his rather dismissive way, but Ella told me he was just the same with her when she started, which I found oddly reassuring given how highly he obviously rates her now. It felt almost like a badge of honour when he bestowed my nickname on me after a couple of weeks, and I rang Ella straight away.

'I'm Flopsy, although he's already shortened it to Flops,' I'd told her.

'Go on. Give me the links,' she'd laughed.

'Beatrice took him to Beatrix Potter. Beatrix Potter wrote Peter Rabbit, whose sisters are Flopsy, Mopsy and Cotton-tail. He said he nearly went from Beatrix Potter to Harry Potter, but Hermione was too much of a mouthful.'

'There are lots of other female characters in Harry Potter. Ginny Weasley, Luna Lovegood, Cho Chang, that French one that nearly drowned in the lake...'

'I'm OK with Flopsy,' I'd told her.

'Is he being nicer to you now?'

'He's never been nasty, just a bit dismissive. But yes, he's perked up. He's actually really good at translating my ideas into instructions for the team to follow.'

'He's a dinosaur, but a benign one on the whole. I'm glad you're getting on better with him.'

'I am.'

Summer is now a long way behind us and the weather has turned, but thankfully the building is watertight again so we're not held up by the rain. All the BudgetWise fixtures and fittings have been consigned to a series of skips, so we're pretty much at the blank canvas stage where we can start to recreate some of The Mermaid's original charm.

'Flops, can I have a word?' John asks after we've concluded the stand-up meeting that Ella suggested we had at the start of each day.

'Sure. What's up?'

'I've been thinking about the floor in the lobby. I know we decided to leave the covering in place to prevent it getting damaged by stuff coming in and out, but we don't actually know what state it's in.'

'You want to lift the plywood and have a look?' I ask.

'We could put it back down afterwards. I'm willing to bet that you can't get those tiles any more, so any broken ones will have to be specially made. Of course, if most of them are broken, we might be looking at a whole new floor, and I'm sure you'd want to know about that sooner rather than later.'

'I wouldn't mind having a look at the mermaid mosaic,' I admit. 'That's going to be a nightmare if it's damaged.'

'Shall I get a couple of chippies to come and lift the floor then?'

'Yes, why not.'

I've never been on an archaeological dig, but the care with which the two woodworkers raise each panel of the plywood covering to reveal the tiled floor underneath reminds me of one. I half expect John to fish out one of those soft brushes and start gently sweeping the dirt off the tiles. There's a gasp of excitement when they raise a panel to reveal a distinctly fishy tail and, by the time the final panel comes up to reveal the mermaid's scantily clad torso and face, it feels like we're all holding our breath.

'That,' observes John softly, 'is a fucking work of art.'

'Mm, I agree. Imagine what it will look like when we've cleaned it up.'

'We'll have to do that anyway, so we can properly see what state the tiles are in. Barry, grab the jet wash, will you?'

'Jet wash'll just fill the place with water, mate,' Barry replies. 'You need to wash the worst of the dirt off by hand and then attack it with one of them rotary cleaners like they have in schools.'

'I'm sure I saw one of those in the store cupboard,' I tell them.

'Looks like you're going to be busy then,' John tells me with a wink. 'I'll get one of the sparkies to check the machine over before you use it. Abby would have my balls for Christmas decorations if I let you electrocute yourself.'

In truth, although I bristle at the assumption that the woman is going to do the menial task, I quite enjoy cleaning the floor. It takes several washes before the worst of the grime is gone, but it's surprisingly rewarding seeing the pattern of the tiles and, more importantly, the mosaic, come back to life. By the time the rotary cleaner has been passed fit for use, the floor is already looking loads better.

'Oi! Where do you think you're going?' I yell as John nonchalantly strides across the lobby on the way to his van at lunchtime, leaving a trail of dusty footprints.

'Oops, sorry, Flops. I'll go out the back way,' he says before retracing his steps, whistling a melody I don't recognise.

'What's the tune?' I call after his retreating form.

'It's from *Calamity Jane*. I can't remember all of it, but basically the theme of the song is about how a woman's touch brightens a home.'

'Very funny,' I tell him sarcastically as I shut the cleaner down and stretch my back.

* * *

By mid-afternoon, the floor is sparkling and John whistles appreciatively when he sees it. 'It's a shame it's going to get mucky again,' he observes. 'But we need it spotless for this. Right, on your knees. You start that side and I'll start over here.'

'What are we doing?' I ask him.

'We're going to go tile by tile, checking for cracks and breaks. Even a hairline crack needs to be investigated. Here, I'll give you a marker so you can mark any affected tiles.'

'Hang on. Are you seriously telling me I've spent hours cleaning this floor just so you can draw on it?'

'Let's just see what we find, shall we?'

Compared to cleaning it, crawling across the floor on my hands and knees inspecting every tile proves to be back-breaking work. By the time John and I finally meet in the middle, my knees and elbows are aching, and my hands are frozen from the cold tiles. The good news is that we've only discovered a couple of cracked tiles near the door, which John thinks will be relatively easy to get out and replace. He's very carefully lifted them out to send to a specialist tiling company, who will hopefully be able to supply matching replacements.

'You should take a picture and send it to Abby,' John suggests. 'I'm sure she'd like to see it before we cover it up again.'

'Good idea,' I tell him as I fish my phone out of my pocket and take several shots from different angles. 'I expect Reginald will be pleased to see it too.'

'Is he the guy in the wedding photos you showed?'

'That's him.'

* * *

It may be only six o'clock when I lock up the site, but I know that's way too late to drop by to see Reginald. The retirement home serves the residents their evening meal at five thirty, and he told me they frown on evening visitors. I'll have to wait until the weekend to show him what we've found. I sent the pictures to Abby though, who replied with a series of love-heart emojis, so I think I can assume she likes it.

I had been worried about telling Reginald about my decision to stay in Margate rather than go chasing after Jock, but he was surprisingly good about it in the end. I have been teasing him a little about his advice to 'hold lightly to things' as he's taken a good deal of interest in the restoration of The Mermaid, and I know he'll be delighted to see that the mosaic is undamaged, despite the havoc BudgetWise wreaked on the rest of the fixtures and fittings.

In fact, and I'm not at all surprised by this, the only real fly in the ointment has been Emilio. He's enthusiastic for the project, but the constant stream of architects, interior designers, kitchen fitters and so on that he's fired at me since coming on board has been a bit of a distraction. I did mention it to Abby during one of her site visits, but she just shrugged and said she'd heard he could be a bit of a diva and not to let it get under my skin. John's summary of the intrusion was rather more pointed.

'I don't see why he keeps sending these useless bloody ponces down from London,' he'd complained last time Abby was here. 'The last one was going on about "recreating the distinctive ambience that lets the customer know they're in a Marcuso's restaurant" or some such bollocks. I told him straight, "Just tell me what colour to paint the sodding walls, OK?" It's nonsense. Do people actually earn a living spouting crap like that?'

The kitchen itself has also been the subject of some heated debate. On his only site visit to date, Emilio declared it 'much too small' and threw a minor tantrum when we explained that the walls were structural and couldn't just be moved around to suit him. At one point, I actually thought he might walk away, but Abby must have found a way to calm him down, because he was perfectly fine the next time I spoke to him.

I haven't heard anything from Jock for a while; I expect he's busy, and I'll confess that I am avoiding him a little. As far as he knows, the Mermaid project is still dead, and maybe the kindest thing is to let him carry on thinking that. The truth won't make him happy at all, so why burden him with it?

29

I'm desperate to show Reginald the picture of the mosaic but, in the end, I don't get time to visit him until Sunday afternoon.

'Hi, Hazel,' I say to the receptionist. 'I'm just popping in to see Reginald.'

'Oh,' she says, and I spot a look of concern on her face. 'Haven't you heard?'

'Heard what?'

'He's not here. He's in hospital.'

'Hospital? Why?' My heart has started thudding uncomfortably in my chest. I know he's old but, apart from being very frail, he's always seemed fine.

'They're doing tests, but it looks like a stroke.'

'When did this happen?'

'This morning. His daughter's with him.'

'Is it serious?'

'When you're Reginald's age, these things are always serious,' she says softly. 'Try not to worry about it, though. He's had a long life, and it's a comparatively kind way to go.'

'He's not dead yet!' I exclaim, horrified.

'Of course not. He might recover, but he'll need a lot more looking after if he does. I'm afraid his needs will be more complex than we'll be able to cope with here.'

I've always liked Hazel, but her defeatist attitude is seriously winding me up.

'You don't know it's a stroke,' I tell her firmly. 'It could be a TIA. My grandad had one of those. Everyone thought it was a stroke but it wasn't and he made a full recovery.'

'You're right,' she says in the kind of soothing voice that lets me know she doesn't share my optimism. 'Let's hope that's it.'

By the time the taxi drops me at the hospital, however, my stomach is churning with anxiety and I'm barely breathing. It takes me a while to find the ward that Reginald is in but, when I do, my worst fears are confirmed. He looks absolutely tiny in the hospital bed; his eyes are closed and there's a monitor next to the bed recording his vital signs.

'You must be Beatrice,' the woman sitting in the chair next to him says quietly. 'I'm Jeannie, Reginald's daughter. He's told me so much about you that it's lovely to meet you in person at last. I just wish it could have been in happier circumstances.' She has a peculiar accent, I notice. Some of her inflections are pure American, but there's the residue of a British accent there too. She's elegantly dressed and, even though she must be well into her sixties, she looks younger. There's a clear family resemblance; she has the same colour eyes as him and I can see hints of him in the shape of her face as well. I turn my attention back to Reginald, who looks so vulnerable; his white hair is spread out on the pillow and his mouth is slack and toothless. If it wasn't for the steady rise and fall of the sheet over his chest, I could believe he was dead. I'm aware of silent tears rolling down my cheeks as I look at him.

'How is he?' I ask, equally quietly.

'It's too early to say. It was a major stroke, they tell me. He's stable at the minute, but very sleepy. He can't speak, but the nurses tell me he should be able to understand, so I've been sitting here talking to him. It sounds a stupid thing to say, but I'm so grateful it happened when I was here. Please, sit down.'

She indicates the visitor chair next to the adjacent bed, which contains a sleeping woman almost as old as Reginald. 'She won't mind,' Jeannie assures me. 'Her visitors have just left. From the look on her face, she was relieved to see them go.'

I pick up the chair and silently move it next to Reginald's bed, taking care not to snag the wires coming out of the monitor. Jeannie is holding one of his hands, but the other is resting on his chest. The skin looks paper thin so I take it in mine gently. It's warm but limp; there's no trace of the fierce grip that he had when he was imploring me to focus on love.

'Talk to him,' Jeannie urges. 'I think I've run out of things to say for now.'

'Hello, Reginald,' I say gently. 'This is Beatrice. Hazel told me you were in here so I came as quickly as I could. You've given us all quite a fright...' My words dry up.

'Tell him about the hotel,' Jeannie suggests. 'He's been so interested in it; he's talked about little else when I've called him.'

'We took up the horrible floor in the lobby,' I continue. 'The original is still there, and it's perfect. The mermaid mosaic looks as good as new.'

Reginald's eyelid twitches.

'We're making really good progress. Do you remember I told you about the retro-style lift that we were going to put in? It's pretty much finished and it looks amazing. Between you and me, Emilio is still being a mighty pain in the arse, though.'

This time, there's no mistaking the reaction. The corner of Reginald's mouth turns up and he squeezes my hand. Jeannie obviously notices too, because she mouths *Keep going* at me. So I carry on chatting to him about everything and nothing. Nearly half an hour passes but there's no further reaction and, after a while, his breathing indicates that he's asleep.

'I expect you think I'm a terrible daughter,' Jeannie murmurs sadly over Reginald's prostrate form. 'His only child living so far away.'

'It's nothing to do with me,' I tell her gently.

'The truth is that I tried to get him to move over so he could be closer to us all after Mum died. But he's a stubborn old mule. I love him to pieces, and I couldn't have asked for better parents, but he made it absolutely clear he wasn't going anywhere. What could I do? My husband, my children and grandchildren are all American.'

'He's very proud of you,' I tell her. 'He's never once said he wished things were any other way. Every time I've visited him, he's told me your latest news. It's funny. This is the first time we've met in person, but in many ways, I feel like I know you already.'

We're still holding Reginald's hands between us, but she lets go and moves her hand so it's on top of mine.

'Thank you,' she says, with a tremor in her voice. I look up to see tears rolling down her cheeks. 'You've been such a good friend to him.'

'He's a good friend to me,' I assure her, as my own tears start to fall again.

We sit there for what feels like an age, either side of Reginald's sleeping body. Although we don't speak, I can feel a silent understanding pass between us. Eventually, the nurse tells us that visiting time is up, and we head for the door together. It turns out that she's rented a flat quite close to the one I'm staying in, so we share a taxi.

'Will you come by and see him again some time?' Jeannie
asks when we pull up outside my flat.

'Of course. I'll come as often as I can.'

'He'll like that. Goodnight, Beatrice.'

'Goodnight, Jeannie.'

* * *

If Monday morning were going to reflect my mood, the sky
would be slate grey and rain would be falling steadily. However,
it's a perfect autumn day, crisp, with a chill in the breeze, but the
sun is shining brightly and there isn't a cloud in the sky.

'Are you all right, Flops?' John asks as we're dealing with a
plumbing issue in one of the bedrooms after the morning stand-
up. 'You don't seem quite yourself today.'

'Sorry. Just got a few things on my mind and I didn't sleep
very well last night. Nothing you need to worry about.'

'Would you like some good news?'

'I always like good news, John. What have you got?'

Before he gets a chance to tell me, we're interrupted by one of
the chippies. 'Sorry to bother you, Beatrice, but there's a woman
outside asking for you.'

I follow him downstairs and my heart breaks as soon as I see
who it is. There's only one reason Jeannie would be here.

'When?' I ask as she wraps me in a surprisingly fierce hug.

'Last night,' she says. 'Barely an hour after we left him.
Another massive stroke. The nurse said it was peaceful, but they
always say that, don't they? I should have been there.'

'You didn't know this was going to happen,' I reassure her
through my tears. 'And maybe he wanted to be alone at the end. I
read an article once that said that some people seem to manage

to hang on until they're alone so they can go quietly without an audience.'

'I'm on my way to collect his things and the paperwork to give to the funeral directors. I know it's an imposition, but would you mind very much coming with me? I'm not sure I can do this on my own.'

'Of course I'll come with you,' I tell her. 'Let me just tell my colleague where I'm going.'

* * *

By the end of the afternoon, I'm wrung out. Little things have set me off all day, like the sight of Reginald's wristwatch among the possessions that the hospital handed over along with the medical certificate detailing the cause of death. I went with Jeannie to register the death at the registry office, and then to the funeral directors that Hazel recommended when we called in at the retirement home to break the news. Standing in his sitting room, where I'd spent so many happy hours drinking tea and chatting with him, was another tearful moment. His 'whizzy' chair looked so sad and forlorn, as if it knew he'd never sit in it again, and that set me off even more.

'I know it's probably way too early to think about this stuff,' Jeannie had said as we'd sat on the sofa together, just letting the emotions pour out, 'but if there's anything you want to take, to remind you of him...'

'You're very kind,' I'd told her.

'I'm not a religious person, particularly, but I like to think he's somewhere up there, reunited with Mum,' she'd said after a long pause. 'He's young again and full of vitality. That's how I want to think of him, anyway.'

'I think you're right,' I'd agreed.

'It's just a shame he'll never see The Mermaid back on its feet. He loved that place.'

'Jeannie,' I'd said as an idea had come to me. 'There is something I'd like, actually, but I don't need it for long.'

'You can have whatever you want, I've already told you that.'

I'd pulled open the drawer where Reginald's wedding album was and turned the pages until I came to the picture of him and Annie standing in the lobby of The Mermaid.

'Can I borrow this picture?' I'd asked. 'I'd like to see if I can get it enlarged and enhanced and then, if you'll give your blessing, I'd like to hang it behind the reception desk when we reopen.'

'I think that's the loveliest idea ever,' she'd told me as she'd gently prised the photo out of its mount.

30

'That looks stunning,' Ella breathes as the last panel of the new reception desk is carefully screwed into place. We're opening in just under a month and the advance bookings are already starting to come in.

'Doesn't it?' I sigh happily. Work on The Mermaid has continued at speed and, to everyone's surprise, we're actually ahead of schedule. It took a bit of negotiation, but in the end I was able to persuade Abby to let me have a brand-new reception desk made in art-deco style. The wood is dark with a deep lustre, and the inlaid brass pattern contrasts with it perfectly. The craftsman who made it also took care to design the desk so that the flatscreen computer monitors will be hidden from the customers' view unless they practically climb over the counter, thus preserving the period feel.

Another little detail that I'm particularly delighted with are the key cards for the rooms. BudgetWise had fitted all the bedroom doors with key-card locks, but the plastic cards just didn't suit the rest of the décor. But, after a lot of head scratching and online research, we've come up with what we think is the best compromise. We have a set of brass keys, each attached to a wooden tag with the room number engraved on it. They will look absolutely in keeping with the rest of the lobby when we hang them on the hooks behind the reception desk. The clever bit is that the wooden tag is actually the key; guests simply need to hold it against the panel on the door to unlock their room.

Across the lobby, the vintage-style lifts are also operational, looking like they've been there since the day the hotel first opened. Sparkling chandeliers hang from the high ceiling, and we've even managed to get a new doorstep installed outside, with *The Mermaid* inlaid in it in brass lettering to add a bit of extra pizzazz. I've spent hours on online auction sites, picking up art-deco knick-knacks for the rooms and public areas. The kitchen is fully installed to Emilio's exact specifications, and he's bringing his team down in a couple of days' time to give it a test run. He's also assured me that the hiring process for the kitchen and dining room is all sorted. I did meet his head of HR, a somewhat frosty woman who made no bones about the fact she considered Margate to be the back of beyond. After no more than ten minutes examining the space, she hotfooted it back to London and we haven't seen her since. Apparently, she conducted all the interviews online. We haven't announced our partnership with Emilio yet, but we've got the press release ready to go. The plan is to drop it just over a week before opening to create an extra buzz.

'Right,' I say to Ella. 'Just one more thing to do.'

I carefully extract the framed picture of Reginald and Annie, hanging it carefully on the wall behind the desk, in a gap specifically left for it.

'That's such a lovely touch,' she tells me. 'Has his daughter gone back to America yet?'

'Yes, she flew out last week. I think she'll be racking up the airmiles while the probate process goes through, but she's packed up his room and got things under way. I never knew there was so much paperwork involved when somebody dies.'

'It's a shame he didn't get a bigger send-off.'

She's right. The attendees at Reginald's funeral consisted of Jeannie, a couple of people from the retirement home and me.

'I think that's probably what happens when you live to that kind of age. Everyone who would normally come to your funeral is already dead.'

Our somewhat maudlin discussion is interrupted by John, who emerges from the lift, holding his phone out in front of him like an unexploded bomb. 'Flops, you need to see this,' he says. 'It's just been on the radio news, and it's breaking online.'

He hands me the phone. The headline of the article is *Famous Chef Arrested*, accompanied by a picture of Emilio. My pulse starts to race as I read the article, holding the phone at an angle so Ella can see it too.

Acclaimed Italian chef Emilio Marcuso, owner of the Marcuso chain of restaurants, was arrested by the Metropolitan police this morning. The charges against him include tax evasion, fraud and modern slavery. Details at this stage are scarce, but it is alleged that Mr Marcuso has employed a number of illegal immigrants in his restaurants, declaring full minimum wage for tax purposes while paying them a fraction of that amount. All Marcuso restaurants were raided in a co-ordinated sting operation involving several police forces and the fraud squad. We will bring you more details as they emerge.

I'm barely at the end of the article before my phone starts ringing. It's Abby, of course, and she's apoplectic.

'Have you seen the bloody news?' she explodes as soon as the call connects.

'John's just shown me the article.'

'Is he there?'

'Yes, Ella too.'

'Put me on speakerphone. We need to brainstorm this.'

I press the button. 'I think we can all agree on the first thing we need to do,' I tell her. 'We need to cut ties with him.'

'Whoa, hang on a minute. What happened to innocent until proven guilty?' Abby asks.

'No smoke without fire,' John replies. 'Big cheese like him, they're going to make sure their case is pretty much watertight before they move.'

'And, from our perspective, it doesn't really matter,' Ella adds. 'He's tainted goods now. Even if he's innocent, people will suspect him. It's not good for brand image.'

'And the last thing we need is my name anywhere near another person accused of wrongdoing,' I tell her.

This does at least make her laugh, albeit grimly.

'What is it with you, hotels and criminals?' she asks.

'Hey, don't pin this on me!' I retort.

'Hm. Tell me, is there anyone in your industry that isn't a crook?'

'Yes. Me, for starters.'

She sighs. 'I know. What are we going to do, though? We'll never get another chef lined up in the time we've got.'

'Push back the opening?' John suggests.

'No. We need to get open and trading,' Abby tells him. 'We've already got advance bookings. It'll do no end of harm if we start cancelling them.'

'Open but without the restaurant at first?' Ella offers.

'But the whole sodding USP was supposed to be the food!'

'OK. Let's step back and try to piece together what we have,' I tell her. 'Point one: Emilio has to go, agreed?'

'Yes.' She sighs again.

'But, in losing Emilio, we also lose all the restaurant staff, because they were employed by him.'

'I'm not sure this is helping my blood pressure,' she complains.

'Hang on.' My brain is starting to recover from the shock, and all sorts of exciting possibilities are opening up. 'He must have recruited locally, because the pay isn't good enough for people to commute long distances.'

'What's your point?' Abby asks. 'If they're all illegals, we can't employ them either.'

'OK, Abby,' I tell her as inspiration finally strikes. 'Here's what I need you to do. Can you get in touch with Emilio's people and find out who he's recruited?'

'What? Are you seriously saying that you want me to call them, tell them we no longer want to be associated with Emilio, but ask if we can use his team anyway? I don't see that one going well.'

'It isn't our fault he got himself arrested. He's given us no choice. As one of the recruitment agents said to me after the whole Hotel Dufour debacle, reputation is everything in this game. I'd go in hard with how he's in breach of the contract and, if he doesn't want us to sue, he needs to give up the team. Something like that. I know you'll be able to pull it off. Channel aggressive Abby.'

'I'm not aggressive!' she protests, causing John and Ella to snort with laughter.

'Assertive then,' I offer.

'Fine. What are you going to do?'

'I'm going to get us a chef.'

* * *

My hands are sweaty as I type out a message to Jock.

> Hi. I need to talk to you. Are you around?

I watch nervously and, to my immense relief, the ticks go blue and I can see he's typing.

> Hi. Busy at the moment but free at 3. Are you OK?

> I'm fine. Talk to you later x.

I try to keep myself busy but time seems to have slowed to a crawl, reminding me of being in the police station waiting for our bail interviews. The biggest problem I have is that I'm going to have to find a way to tell Jock that the project is still going, and come up with a reasonable explanation about why I didn't tell him, and why he hasn't heard anything from me for so long. In the end, I decide that I need to tell him the truth. If I fudge this, and he finds out later, it's going to be much worse than being upfront with him.

'Hi,' he says when the video call connects.

'Hi yourself,' I reply. My heart is suddenly thudding in my chest and my stomach is a mass of nervous butterflies. I feel much more like a schoolgirl talking to her crush than a hotel director speaking to a potential colleague, and the whole sensation has caught me completely unaware. Meanwhile, the silence is starting to feel oppressive.

'How are you?' Jock asks cautiously.

'Yeah, good. You?' *Come on, Beatrice. This is agony.*

'I'm OK, thanks. You said you needed to talk to me,' he prompts.

'That's right.' I seize the mental lifeline with both hands.

'Look, I'm sorry I haven't been in touch lately. So much has been happening that my feet have hardly touched the ground.'

'That's OK. What have you been up to?'

I take a deep breath and launch into the story, explaining about how the project was resurrected, but carefully leaving out Emilio for now. Any guilt I feel about not being completely truthful, like I'd planned, is overruled by the fact that I don't want to hurt his feelings by making him think he wasn't the first choice.

'In fact, that's why I'm calling. I've got a job opening that I wanted to run past you, to see if you were interested,' I tell him at the end.

'I see,' he says after a pause. Am I imagining it, or has his tone of voice changed? He certainly doesn't look happy now. Have I gone about this the wrong way? Once more, I find myself paralysed.

'Why don't you tell me about it,' he suggests after a while.

'It's the same as we talked about before. The head chef position here at The Mermaid.'

'Starting when?'

'The middle of next month.'

There's another long pause.

'Hm.'

'What?' I ask.

'I know you, Beatrice. There's no way you'd get this close to the wire with such a key position unfilled, especially when you told me last time we spoke that food was the USP and you even got me to design a menu. There's something you're not telling me.'

Shit. Maybe I should have been up front about Emilio from the start after all. He looks really pissed off now. I'm losing him, I can tell, and I need to turn this conversation around fast. 'Fine, full disclosure. I wanted you from the beginning, as you know, but Abby, my co-director, wanted a name, so she forced this celebrity chef on me.'

'Who?'

'Emilio Marcuso.'

'The one that's just been arrested.'

'You've heard then?'

'Incredibly, we have news in Scotland.' His voice is dripping with sarcasm. 'You are a piece of work, you know that?'

'What are you talking about?'

'Stupidly, I thought you actually wanted to talk to me because you cared about me.'

'I do!'

'You don't. All you care about is your precious hotel. Face it, the only reason you called me is because you're in a hole. What would have happened if Emilio hadn't got arrested? I probably wouldn't have heard from you again.'

'That's not true!' I blurt. 'I had a plan, actually...'

But it's too late. I'm talking to a blank screen. Jock has gone and I know, without a doubt, that I've just made the biggest mistake of my life. I look around the lobby of the hotel, but all the excitement I normally feel about this place has gone. I should never have allowed Abby and Christopher to railroad me into accepting Emilio. I'm supposed to be the expert; neither of them knows the first thing about hospitality. I should have fought harder for Jock and, crucially, I should never have kept him in the dark. Yes, my intentions were good, but the result is just the same. I've betrayed him, and he has every right to be angry with me. Hot tears are pouring down my cheeks now. How the hell am I going to fix this?

31

By the time I wake from a restless night, just after five the next morning, I know what I have to do. I did call Jock several more times yesterday evening but, unsurprisingly, I always got diverted to voicemail. I messaged him too, telling him I was sorry, but I can see the messages are still unread this morning. If he won't speak to me on the phone, I'll have to go and see him face to face. I can't leave things like this.

By seven o'clock, I'm on my way to the airport and I reckon it's safe to call Abby without waking her. I can't tell her I'm bunking off to try to fix my relationship with Jock, but if I make it about him professionally, she won't have an issue. That's my plan, anyway.

'Hi. How are you getting on?' she asks. I can tell from the background noise that she's not at home either.

'I'm going to Scotland,' I tell her. 'The chef is playing hard to get. Are you OK with that? I shouldn't be away for more than a day or two and John's got everything under control.'

'Yeah, no worries.' She sounds deflated.

'Where are you?' I ask.

'On the train to London. I can't get anyone at Emilio's company to answer the phone, so I'm going to show up in person and refuse to leave until they talk to me. I'll keep you posted, yeah?'

'OK. Good luck.' My mind is cast back to the night I was arrested, where I took the phone off the hook to stop the journalists from getting through. I wonder if Emilio's team are doing the same. Thinking of that night takes me down a rabbit hole. I'm reminded of Jock letting me share his bed when I was scared, how safe I felt with him, and how he just seemed to be able to read me like a book. I let the mental images play in my mind as I pull out my phone and look at a few of the photos from our week together. I may have given Abby the impression that this trip was purely business, but the reality is I'm not even thinking about The Mermaid at the moment. This is all about Jock and me, and putting things right. I have no idea how long it's going to take, so I've packed a small overnight case. Hopefully, I'll be able to find a hotel or B&B if I need to stay over. One thing is for sure: I'm not coming back until this is straightened out. If Jock doesn't want to come and work at The Mermaid, that's fine. I mean, it's not fine but I'm sure we'll find a way around it. What I absolutely cannot cope with is the idea of him thinking badly of me.

* * *

'Can you take me to Gregory's restaurant in the city centre?' I ask the taxi driver as I bundle myself into the cab.

He turns round and stares at me disbelievingly. 'Really?'

'Yes. Why?'

'I'm just trying to work out what kind of person would get on a plane to come to Gregory's. Where have you come from?'

'London.'

'Wow. I mean, it's OK, but I wouldn't cross the city to go there, let alone the country.'

'Just take me. Please?'

'You're the boss.'

As we join the motorway heading for the city, I try to fit the taxi driver's description of Gregory's with what Jock told me. I guess a posh, old-school establishment isn't to everybody's taste, but that wasn't the impression the driver was giving off. Maybe there are two Gregory's, and there's been some sort of mix-up. This is confirmed when he turns onto a shabby street and pulls up outside a greasy spoon café that looks like it's seen better days.

'Here you are.'

'I'm sorry,' I tell him. 'There must be some mistake. I meant the other Gregory's.'

'I've lived here all my life,' he replies. 'This is the only Gregory's. Do you want me to wait while you check it out?'

'Would you?'

'No skin off my nose. The meter's running.'

'Thanks.' I get out of the taxi and push open the door of the café. It may look run down on the outside, but it's obviously popular, as most of the tables are busy.

'Find a seat,' the guy behind the counter tells me. 'I'll be with you in a minute.'

'I'm not here for food, actually. I'm looking for someone. This is probably mad, but does Andrew McLaughlin work here?'

I'm expecting a flat no but, to my surprise, the man turns and yells in the direction of the kitchen.

'Andy, there's someone here to see you.'

After a moment, Jock appears, and my heart goes into my mouth. He's hot, sweaty and a little dishevelled but he looks absolutely perfect to me.

'Who is it?' he begins before doing a double-take as his eyes meet mine. 'What are you doing here?' he asks. He doesn't look pleased to see me.

'Since you won't answer my calls or reply to my messages, you didn't leave me much choice,' I tell him, trying to keep the tremor out of my voice. I'm aware that my hands are sweating and I can feel the heat as a hot flush spreads across my chest and up my neck. I probably look like some kind of beacon but I don't care.

'I'm working,' he says flatly and starts to turn away.

'I'm not going anywhere,' I call after him. 'I'll sit here all day if I have to.'

'It's a free country,' he replies and disappears back into the kitchen.

'You'll need to order something if you're going to take up a table,' the man behind the counter tells me, obviously enjoying my discomfort.

'OK,' I reply. 'What's good?'

'The Olympic all-day breakfast is our most popular.'

'I'll have one of those then.'

'Grand. Tea or coffee?'

'I don't suppose there's any chance of a flat white?'

'No. Tea or coffee?'

'Tea please.'

'White or brown toast?'

'I don't need toast.'

'It comes with the breakfast.'

'Fine. Brown please.'

'Great. Grab a seat and I'll get that on for you.'

'I'm just going to nip out and pay the cab driver first, OK?'

'I'll need to take payment if you're stepping outside. Company policy.'

'Listen,' I tell him forcefully. 'I've been up since God knows when. It's taken two trains, an aeroplane and a taxi to get here, just to talk to your mate Andy. Do you seriously think I'm going to do a runner to get out of paying for, how much is the breakfast?'

'Ten ninety-nine, and your life story doesn't change company policy. Card or cash?'

I hand over my card with a growl and, after settling up with the taxi driver, take a seat at one of the vacant tables. A few minutes pass before the guy from behind the counter saunters over with a steaming mug of tea and some cutlery. From the ambience of the place, I'm expecting something with the vague flavour of dishwater, but this is surprisingly good. It's proper builders' tea: strong and milky. John would approve, I decide. He'd also doubtless approve of the Olympic all-day breakfast, although I'm overwhelmed by the sheer size of it. Everything seems to be doubled; there are two eggs, two sausages, two rashers of bacon, two hash browns, two grilled tomatoes, two slices of black pudding, a small lake of baked beans and a pile of button mushrooms all crammed onto an enormous plate. I'd struggle to eat half of this in normal circumstances; with my anxiety about what to say to Jock affecting my appetite, I doubt I'll manage a quarter. Things go from bad to worse when the server brings another plate with four slices of thickly buttered brown toast. Just looking at all this food is making me feel queasy.

Remembering Jock's words about using the carbs to soak up the egg, I cut a corner off one of the hash browns and pierce one of the yolks with it. It's comfort food of the first order, and I follow it up with a bit of sausage. This proves to be a mistake; the sausage is well cooked, but obviously cheap as the filling is fatty and flavourless. I add a little brown sauce, mixing it with some beans and a bit of bacon. That's much better. The bacon is cooked just right; the fat is rendered without the meat being charred to a crisp. In the end, I manage nearly a third of the breakfast before pushing the plate away in defeat.

'Was the breakfast not to your taste?' the man from behind the counter asks as he clears away my plate.

'It was lovely,' I tell him. 'There was just rather a lot of it.'

'You didn't touch your toast.' He sounds mildly affronted, as if I've insulted him personally in some way.

'I did tell you I didn't want it,' I explain.

'No alterations to the menu items,' he states firmly. 'Company policy.'

'I see. Tell me, who sets the policy?'

'I do. I'm Gregory, the owner.'

'Right. Don't you think a little flexibility might have served you well here, Gregory? I mean, I told you I didn't want the toast but, because of your inflexible policy, you're now going to have to throw it away when you could have saved yourself some money by simply not serving it in the first place.'

'No.'

'No?'

'No. If I start allowing people to change things or swap things around, it all gets in a mess. So, you don't want the toast. I say, "Fine, don't have the toast," but then you'll say, "I'm not paying £10.99 because I didn't have the toast." Or you tell me you want to swap an egg for an extra sausage. Sausages are way more expensive than eggs. It all becomes a nightmare. The Olympic breakfast is what it is. Same with every other dish on the menu. No variation, no argument. Everyone has an easy life. Have you finished your tea?'

'Yes, thank you. I'll just sit and wait for Jock now.'

'Umm, no.'

'What?'

'If you're occupying a table, you have to order something.'

'I did.'

'Yes, but you've finished. So now you either have to leave or order something else.'

'Are you for real?'

'It's company policy.'

'For fuck's sake. OK, I'll have another cup of tea, please.'

'We don't sell tea on its own. It only comes with a meal.'

'But I don't want a meal! I've just had a bloody meal.'

'And I need to make a living. How long does it take to drink a cup of tea? Fifteen, maybe twenty minutes? Half an hour at a push. You're occupying a table for four for half an hour; I need more return than the price of a single cup of tea.'

'Let me guess. Company policy?'

'Yup.'

'Fine. What's the smallest meal that comes with a cup of tea?'

'That would be our regular breakfast. Seven ninety-nine.'

'Right. I'll have one of those then.'

'I need to take payment up front.'

'Why? I'm literally sitting here, Gregory. I'm not leaving the building.'

'Yes, but I believe you to be a hostile customer, and company policy states that we take payment up front from hostile customers.'

'You are unbelievable,' I tell him as I follow him to the counter and hand over my card.

'Just trying to make a living,' he replies. 'Take a seat and I'll bring your order out as soon as it's ready.'

By the time my second breakfast arrives, the café is almost empty. The tea is still welcome, but I leave the food to congeal on the plate. There's no way I could eat another thing, but I've decided to play Gregory at his own game. After twenty minutes or so, he comes back, but this time I'm ready for him.

'Shall I take your plate?' he asks.

'No. I haven't finished.'

'But it'll be cold by now.'

'Is there anything in your company policy that states what temperature the food needs to be when I eat it?'

'No, but...' He peters out and I decide to press home my victory.

'Your policy is that I have to order something if I'm to occupy a table. I'm occupying a table and I've ordered something, so I'm within policy. I'll let you know when I've finished.'

After another fifteen minutes, he's practically twitching with frustration. I'm pretending to look at my phone, but keeping an eye on him at the same time, so I spot him crossing the floor towards me.

'I still haven't finished,' I tell him without looking up.

'Ah, come on,' he whines. 'You're obviously not going to eat it.'

'Company policy doesn't say I have to eat it. It just says I have to order it. As long as it's there, I can occupy this table, isn't that right?'

'Technically, yes,' he says with a sigh. 'But surely you can see this isn't in the spirit of what's meant.'

'I'm just playing by the rules, Gregory, same as you. Does company policy dictate how long I have to finish my breakfast?'

'No, but...'

'Right then. I'm still eating, and I'll let you know when I'm done.'

'We close at three.'

'I'll make sure I'm done by then.'

32

By the time three o'clock comes around, the standoff between me and Gregory is reaching epic proportions. He keeps looking at me, and I can practically hear his brain whirring as he tries to find some piece of his fabled company policy to use against me, but I'm losing interest in him. It was a fun game while it lasted, but my mind is now firmly back on the main task: Operation Get Jock To Speak To Me.

'We're closed,' Gregory announces triumphantly as he swoops in to clear my plate.

'Great. I'll just wait for Jock, I mean Andrew, and then I'll be out of your hair.'

'Andy?' he says with a malicious smile. 'He left half an hour ago when the kitchen closed. Why didn't you say you were waiting for him?'

'You knew full well I was bloody waiting for him!' I exclaim.

'Did I?' he asks innocently. 'I must have forgotten. Anyway, he doesn't want to talk to you. Forcing him to spend time with you against his will constitutes harassment, and I'm sure it won't surprise you to know that's against company policy.'

'You're enjoying this, aren't you?'

'It's livened up an otherwise ordinary day, yes. Would you like me to call a taxi to take you back to the airport?'

'No.'

'Really?'

'Yes. One, you'd probably charge me for doing it, and two, I'm not going anywhere until I speak to Andrew. I will come back here every day, and not eat as many breakfasts as it takes, until I speak to him. What time do you open?'

'Seven o'clock, but—'

'But nothing. Expect me at seven for the regular breakfast. I eat quite slowly, I'm afraid, so it might take me until three to finish it. I'll be back every day at the same time until I get to speak to him. Just so you know.'

'You wouldn't,' Gregory scoffs, but I can see the doubt in his eyes.

'She would,' a familiar voice says from the kitchen doorway.

'What are you doing here, Andy?' Gregory asks, clearly baffled. 'I thought you'd gone home.'

'I set off for home, but then I realised something,' Jock tells him.

'What?'

'That Beatrice would do exactly what she's doing. The only way to get rid of her is for me to talk to her, so I came back. Hello, Beatrice.'

'Hello, Jock,' I reply as coolly as I can. This is difficult when most of my internal organs are doing a victory dance and singing, *He came back! He came back!*

* * *

After we leave a still bewildered Gregory to lock up the café, Jock leads me in silence down several roads until we reach a small park. I follow him inside, where he slumps onto the first vacant bench. I perch myself carefully beside him and let the silence settle over us. Although I have about a thousand questions, starting with what the hell he's doing working in a greasy spoon café for a man like Gregory, I need to let him go at his pace, I realise.

'Why are you here?' he asks eventually. His voice is flat and lifeless.

'I told you. It was the only way I could find to talk to you after you stopped taking my calls.'

'But I don't want to talk to you, Beatrice. That's why I stopped taking your calls, don't you see?'

'I know, and I'm sorry. Really properly sorry, Jock. I didn't want Emilio, but it was two against one.'

'It's not just that.'

'What is it then? Tell me, Jock.'

He sighs so deeply, it's like he has the whole world on his shoulders.

'Do you remember,' he begins eventually, 'that first night at Hotel Dufour after we were arrested?'

'Vividly,' I tell him.

'Before that night, I saw you as little more than a career-obsessed automaton, like the majority of our clientele. But you were so different when we came back from the police station. You were funny and human, and that week we spent together was amazing.'

'I enjoyed it too. All of it.'

'The point is that you got in my head, Beatrice. I tried not to let you because I knew we were time limited, but you did and I couldn't stop thinking about you after we split up. I'd wake up wondering what you were doing and think about you throughout the day. I knew it was futile and not good for me, that you'd moved on and that was that. I kept telling myself to pull myself together and let you go, but it didn't work. And then I saw you on TV, and you looked so amazing, I couldn't help but send you a message, even though the rational part of me knew I'd never be able to heal and move on if I kept picking at the wound.'

'I loved hearing from you.'

'I used to entertain this fantasy in my head that maybe you felt the same as I did. I knew it was nonsense; all the evidence showed you were getting on with your life, putting your career back on track and all the stuff I knew you would do, but sometimes I'd allow myself to daydream that you were missing me, thinking of me like I was thinking about you.'

'I was!'

'Yeah, well,' he says bitterly.

'I'm not following you, Jock,' I tell him.

'When you messaged me yesterday, you said you wanted to talk. Maybe it was stupid, maybe I read more into it than I should have. Well, I *obviously* read more into it than I should have, because I let myself believe that you were going to tell me something important. Something about you and me. Then you called, and it wasn't you.'

'Of course it was me!'

'It wasn't. It was the other Beatrice, in career mode, with her automaton career voice, offering me a job. Oh, and not because she actually wanted me, but only because she was desperate after the celebrity chef she'd chosen first went and got himself arrested. That's when the scales fell from my eyes, and I saw that the Beatrice I'd fallen for wasn't real. The real one is the one I knew and didn't much like before we were arrested. That's why I'm angry, and that's why I don't want to talk to you. I can see I've been an idiot; I really don't want you in my face to show me how much of an idiot I've been.'

I'm staggered, and for a moment I can't think of anything to say.

'I think we're finished here. Have a safe trip back to London,' Jock says, getting to his feet. This is enough to spur me into action.

'Sit down,' I tell him fiercely. He's hit a nerve, and I'm angry now.

'Why?'

'Because you don't get to lay a truckload of shit like that on me without having the decency to hear what I have to say in return. At least, the Jock I thought I knew would never do that.'

He sighs and sits back down.

'Right,' I begin. 'First things first. You got in my head too, Jock. Like you, I tried to move on, but you were always there. Even when I was busy, you were in the background. When you texted me in Mallorca, I can't tell you how much it meant to me to know that you were still thinking of me. But, like you, I've tried to be realistic. Everything you said led me to believe that you were happy up here, that you were working in a top-class restaurant and moving on with your life. What the hell is the deal with Gregory's, anyway?'

'It's a long story.'

'Hm. Anyway, all the vibes I was getting from you were that you'd settled and moved on. I spent hours analysing every conversation we'd had, trying to pick up the faintest clue that you felt the same as me, but there was nothing. Not a thing. I was happy for you, Jock, and I tried to do the same. But when The Mermaid project came up, I'll admit I had my own daydream. In my dream, you and I were working together, doing what we do best and making a success of it. But it was much more than that. I had a fantasy, just as stupid as yours, that we would also be together again, but without any time limits.'

'It can't have been that important a dream if you promptly signed up the first celebrity chef that walked past.'

'Have you listened to a word I've said? You were *always* my first choice, Jock. If the decision had been mine, I'd have been on the phone straight away. But it isn't. I have business partners, and they overruled me. I tried to tell them that Margate wouldn't be taken in by a cynical marketing ploy, but they felt Emilio would help to fill the place from day one, and you wouldn't because nobody knew who you were.'

'They've got a point,' he concedes. 'Emilio does have a big following. At least, he *did*.'

'Exactly. So, reluctantly, I went with the flow. Then Emilio got himself arrested and I seized the opportunity to revert to my original plan. I was so excited about speaking to you, and then it all went horribly wrong. I mean it when I say I'm sorry, Jock. I made a huge mess, but this isn't about The Mermaid. It's about you and me. Yes, I admit that I want you to come and cook at The Mermaid, because you're a brilliant chef, but there's much more to it than that. I'm going on an incredible adventure and I want to share it with you. Don't you see, Jock? Career Beatrice and the Beatrice you say you fell for aren't different people. I'm both of them, only not the automaton part. It's not wrong to want to be good at what I do for work, but I'm still the Beatrice you say you fell for as well. I'm sorry for making such a mess of everything but I want to try to put it right, even if you decide you don't want to come on the adventure with me. Because I care about you, Jock. You're an incredible man and nobody has ever got me the way you do.'

He turns to look at me and I try to read his expression, but it's inscrutable. I'm desperate for him to say something, anything.

'I see you're wearing your hair up again,' he observes eventually.

'What's that got to do with anything?'

'I always saw it as a metaphor.'

'*What?*'

'Hair up meant career mode. I fell for you when you let your hair down.'

'Sorry, Jock, but that's total bollocks. I put my hair up automatically at the moment because I've been working on a building site, among lots of machinery that would happily take my head off if loose hair got tangled in it. Look.' I reach behind my head, yanking out the pins and the doughnut to let my hair fall loose around my shoulders. 'Is that better?'

He smiles. God, I love his smile, and I was seriously starting to think I'd never see it again. 'Have I been a bit of a dick?' he asks.

'No. Well, maybe just a little bit. But if anyone is the dick here, it's me for not telling you the truth in the first place. I really am sorry.'

'Can I ask you a question?'

'Sure.'

'Did you really daydream about me?'

'More than you can imagine.'

'Why didn't you tell me how you felt?'

'Why didn't you? And, while I'm thinking about it, why did you tell me that Gregory's was an upmarket restaurant?'

'I didn't. You jumped to that conclusion and it suited me not to correct you. It's not exactly the career path I dreamed of, and I was embarrassed.'

'Why are you working for him?'

He sighs. 'I found out I was basically unemployable up here. Head-chef positions don't come up very often, and nobody would take me on as a sous chef because I'd been a head chef before. Chefs are a paranoid bunch; you don't want someone under you who's used to being in charge, is possibly more capable than you and is definitely after your job. So, I hawked myself around, aiming lower and lower, until eventually Gregory took me on.'

'I really don't like him.'

'He's OK, actually. Yes, he's a bit inflexible and he does like to spout his company-policy line, but he's not a bad guy to work for.'

Silence falls again, but there's no tension in it now. We're both lost in our thoughts. After a while, his hand reaches out and takes mine. I savour the warmth of it, enjoying the effect the physical contact is having on me.

'What happens now?' I ask eventually, hoping he hasn't noticed the slight tremble in my voice.

'I don't know. What do you want to happen?'

'In my fantasy, this is the part where you'd take me in your arms and tell me you were never going to let me go again. We catch the next plane to London together and live happily ever after in this beautiful hotel by the sea.'

'I can't come to London with you on the next plane,' he says softly.

'It's OK. I understand. What do we do about you and me, though? I can't just walk away from you again.'

'Beatrice, shut up for a minute. I can't come with you because I need to tie up a couple of loose ends here before I fly south. I need to let Gregory know, give notice to my landlady, those kinds of boring things. When did you say you were opening?'

'Three and a half weeks from today.'

'Bloody hell. I'll be down by the weekend then. Gregory's going to hit the roof, but I assume you don't need a reference from him anyway.'

'Are you serious?'

'Absolutely.'

He stands, takes my hands in his and pulls me to my feet before wrapping me gently in his arms, tightening his grip as I fold myself into his embrace. I'd forgotten how this felt and I turn my head so I can listen to the reassuring thump-thump-thump of his heart. 'I don't ever want to let you go,' he says, 'but I'm going to have to, just for the next few days. What time's your flight, by the way?'

'I haven't booked one yet,' I say. 'I wasn't sure how long I'd need to be up here.'

'Stay the night,' he urges. 'Please?'

I pull my head back so I can look into his eyes. 'Why would I do that?' I ask with a smile.

He smiles back. Did I mention that I love his smile? 'We still haven't worked out who the phantom spooner is,' he replies simply.

EPILOGUE

It's going to be a beautiful day. I can tell because, although it's not yet six in the morning, the sunlight is streaming through a tiny chink in our thick bedroom curtains. Beside me, Jock appears to be fast asleep, although the way he opens his eyes and stares at me when I gently brush his lips with mine indicates that he's probably been awake for a while, the same as me. Even though we've been working and living together for six months now, I still have to pinch myself sometimes when I wake up and see him lying next to me. Abby was initially sceptical about hiring what she saw as an unknown, but I put my foot down this time, and she changed her tune pretty quickly after she tasted his food. After a lot of legal threatening on both sides, Emilio's company agreed to sign over the staff they'd hired, but it turned out that Abby had an even better trick up her sleeve, namely Flo. It was Flo who got the word out among her influencer buddies, and between them they generated a real buzz online about McLaughlin at The Mermaid. The restaurant is now fully booked weeks in advance for both lunch and dinner, although not today because it's closed for a very special function.

'Cup of tea?' I ask.

He smiles. 'Is that "Would you like a cup of tea, Jock" or "Would you get me a cup of tea, Jock"?'

'The first, actually, but don't let me stop you if you prefer the second.'

He stretches luxuriantly and yawns. 'It's OK, I don't mind making it. You stay here and run through all the lists in your head another time.'

'What do you mean?'

'I can practically hear your brain whirring. How much sleep do you think you got?'

'Not much,' I admit. 'A couple of hours, maybe.'

'You'll be fine, you know that don't you? It's not like this is the first wedding reception we've done here.'

'You're right, but these aren't just any guests. I want it to be as perfect as it can be for Ella and Noah.'

'If something goes wrong, we'll deal with it like we always do.'

'And how's that?'

'Fudge it like mad and hope they don't notice,' he says with a grin as he swings his legs out of the bed and stands up, peering carefully out of the curtains. 'They've lucked out with the weather,' he observes.

Although I'm mildly annoyed that he's read me so easily, I do love how well he knows me, I reflect as I allow my brain to run through the mental checklists for the umpteenth time. The wedding is at one, and they're taking pictures in various locations afterwards. All being well, we're expecting them to arrive at around three thirty, when we'll serve welcome drinks and canapés on the beach and also check in the guests who are staying overnight. They'll be sitting down for the wedding break-fast at four, which is the point that I will hopefully be able to start to relax as they'll be Jock's responsibility from then until the end of the party at midnight.

Even though I trust the housekeeping staff implicitly, I'm still going to check every room forensically before the wedding guests arrive to make sure that everything is exactly how I'd expect it to be. Ella dropped off her and Noah's overnight stuff yesterday; they're going to go back home before heading off on honeymoon to Crete on Monday so it was just a small bag of essentials. I've suggested to her that any other guests who are passing on the way to the wedding can also drop their luggage beforehand to save dragging it in through a throng of wedding and other hotel guests later.

'How are the lists shaping up?' Jock asks as he hands me a mug of tea.

'I think they're all right. A few things to do. What about you?'

'I'm pretty happy. They're all dishes we know, so we should be good.'

'Have you got enough time after the breakfast service to prep?'

'Relax. We prepped as much as we could yesterday, so hopefully there isn't that much to do.'

'You sound so calm. Aren't you nervous at all?'

'Of course I'm nervous! I want it to go well just as much as you do.'

'It's funny,' I muse as I sit up and take a sip of my tea. 'Do you remember talking about our dreams when we were in London? Who'd have thought that we'd end up here?'

'Here is better than my dreams,' he says.

'You sound very sure.'

'I am.' He leans forward and kisses me. 'My original dream didn't have you in it. What about you? Still hankering after that country-house hotel?'

'Nah. This is better.'

'Because it has me in it?' he prompts.

'You're incidental,' I tell him with a laugh. 'It's Margate I've fallen in love with.'

'Ouch,' he says, clutching his chest dramatically.

'Of course it's better because you're in it,' I tell him. 'I love you. You know that.'

'It never hurts to hear it again.'

When the guests start to file into the lobby a little after half-past three, my nerves dissipate instantly as I swing into action, issuing room keys, relieving people of their luggage and supervising the distribution of drinks and canapés. Ella and Noah are the last to arrive; she looks absolutely radiant in a simple but elegant wedding dress that flatters her figure beautifully, although I can't help wondering with a smile whether she's wearing her steel-toe-capped builder's boots underneath it. Seeing Noah in a suit is also a surprise, although not as much as seeing John in one. He doesn't look entirely comfortable in it and keeps tugging at the collar of his white shirt. The reason quickly becomes obvious; the way his neck is spilling over the top of it means it must be at least one size too small.

'Is it a bit tight?' I murmur as I hand over their room key.

'Fucking strangling me, Flops,' he murmurs back.

'I reckon, now that the service and photos are done, you could undo the top button of your shirt,' I tell him. 'You'd be a lot more comfortable.'

'That might be true, but that doesn't solve the problem with the ones over my stomach,' he complains. 'I thought they were going to ping off when I was sitting down in the church earlier. I must have put a bit of weight on since the last time I wore this shirt. How I'm going to make it through the wedding breakfast without accidentally exposing myself is anyone's guess.'

'I said you should have tried it on before today, didn't I?' his wife scolds mildly. 'I could have got you another one.'

'Yeah, well,' he replies. 'There's nothing that can be done about it now.'

'I wouldn't be so sure,' I offer.

'Are you going to tell me you've got a stash of white shirts hidden away somewhere?' he asks.

'No. But part of my job is knowing how to solve problems like this. Come with me.'

I lead him into the office behind the reception desk and, after a quick internet search and a couple of calls, a fresh shirt in a larger size is making its way in a taxi from one of the menswear shops in town. When it arrives, a few minutes later, I leave him in peace to get changed and I'm relieved when he reappears with a smile on his face.

'Better?' I ask.

'Much. I tell you what. You're quite good at this hospitality gig, Flops.'

'Praise indeed.' I laugh. 'Now, go and have fun.'

After a while, the guests are called into the dining room to take their places and await the bride and groom. The lobby empties swiftly and soon it's just Ella, Noah and me left in there.

'Thank you again for this,' Ella says. 'I can't believe Atkinsons are picking up the tab either.'

I smile as I glance up at the picture of Reginald and Annie above the reception desk. 'It's company policy to contribute to employee weddings.'

'We're ready for you now,' the MC interrupts, cutting off further explanation.

I hover in the doorway as the MC announces Ella and Noah and the dining room erupts with applause. Once they're seated, the service starts and appears to flow seamlessly. After the main courses have gone out, I risk stepping into the kitchen to check up on Jock.

'All OK?' I ask him.

'Yup. A couple of glitches, but nothing serious. How's it looking out there?'

'Everyone looks like they're having a great time. James's wine choices seem to be going down well too, if the number of empty bottles stacking up is anything to go by.'

'That man is a walking encyclopaedia of wine. I'm so glad we've got him on board. Do you think he and Abby will marry?'

'I wouldn't be surprised. They're very different, but they seem to work really well together.'

'What about us? Could you see yourself married to me?'

'What brought that on?'

'I don't know. We've talked a lot about commitment, but never marriage. I was just interested, I suppose.'

'So it's a hypothetical question,' I clarify.

'As opposed to?'

'A proposal.'

He thinks for a long time before replying.

'I think it depends on your answer,' he says. 'If it's no, then it was a hypothetical question and I'll never mention it again. If the answer is yes, however...'

'And they said romance was dead.' I laugh, before clocking the expression on his face. 'Oh God, you're serious, aren't you?'

'I wasn't to begin with, but it seems to have gone there. Will you marry me, Beatrice? I realise this is a bit sudden, and probably not the most romantic environment, so I'll understand if you need time to think.'

I look around the pristine kitchen. Nobody has noticed our conversation; everybody is concentrating on their work, but I realise something.

'It's the perfect location,' I tell him. 'Right in the beating heart of our favourite place in the world. I'd love to marry you.'

'Really?'

'Were you expecting me to say no?'

'No, I guess... Oh, wow! I really want to kiss you right now, but I don't think the food hygiene people would like it.'

'Kiss me later. I'd better get back.'

I'm in a daze as I wander back to the dining room. Did that really just happen? Somehow, I'd always expected it to be a magically romantic moment when someone proposed to me, rather than a curious question over the kitchen pass that escalated rapidly. As I think about it more, however, I realise that it's typical of us. He did catch me by surprise, but once I'd got over the initial shock, it was totally obvious what my answer would be. Doing my best to snap back into work mode, I cast my eyes automatically around the guests to check if anyone needs help. Ella and Noah look as happy as songbirds, chatting with the other people on the top table. Abby is deep in conversation with James on one of the other tables, while her father chats easily with the woman on his left. John is looking relaxed and gives me a little wave when he spots me. I'm feeling stupidly happy, and it takes me a minute to realise I'm not alone.

'This is superb,' Flo tells me. 'I mean, I knew it would be, but I just thought I'd tell you anyway. How's it all going? You look pleased.'

'I am, but that's not why I'm smiling. Jock just proposed.'

'*What??*' She looks outraged.

'Is it bad form to propose at someone else's wedding?' I ask, trying to work out what she's so upset about.

'No, it's not that. It's just seriously off to propose when you're both working. He could have taken you out for dinner at least.'

'I think it was a spur-of-the-moment thing. It's fine.'

She's silent for a moment. 'Can I be a bridesmaid?' she asks. 'I've loved being a bridesmaid for Abby.'

'Of course.' I laugh. 'You and Abby and Ella can all be bridesmaids if you like.'

She grabs me in a fierce hug. 'I'm so happy for you. I'd better get back to my duties.'

I glance around the room once more, smiling as I catch various people's eyes. I've always accepted that loneliness comes with the territory in a job like mine, and it was a sacrifice I made happily for the work that I love. Now, however, standing in the dining room of my own hotel, surrounded by people who have become close friends and with the man I love so much just the other side of the pass, I realise that I don't need to make that sacrifice any more. I thought I'd always miss the bright lights of London, but I don't.

This is where I belong, and exactly where I want to be. The man of my dreams has just proposed. And, hopefully, somewhere up there, Reginald is cheering us on.

ACKNOWLEDGEMENTS

Thank you so much for reading this book, and I hope you enjoyed Beatrice and Jock's story. If you've read my previous book, *Love at First Site*, I hope you also enjoyed catching up with Abby, Ella, Noah and John once more.

Richard, thank you for your help on the police procedures; hopefully I've got them right. I think it's safe to say that this book had something of a difficult birth, so I want to say a special thank you to my editor, Rachel, who ended up having to do two full rounds of structural edits. The story is much better for your input, so thank you for sticking with it and being so patient with me.

Massive thanks as always to the rest of the incredible Boldwood team. Thank you to Emily for copy editing once again, and Jennifer for proof reading. Of course, getting the story as good as it can be is just the beginning, and I want to say thank you also to Amanda, Nia, Jenna and all the team for the incredible work you do to connect my books with readers.

Mandy, thank you for your alpha reading and encouragement once again.

Final thank yous, as always, go to my family, who could not be more supportive and give me time to write. Thanks also to Bertie the Labradoodle, my patient companion on plotting walks.

ABOUT THE AUTHOR

Phoebe MacLeod is the author of several popular romantic comedies including the top ten bestseller, *The Fixer Upper*. She lives in Kent with her partner, grown up children and disobedient dog.

Sign up to Phoebe MacLeod's mailing list here for news, competitions and updates on future books.

Follow Phoebe on social media:

X x.com/macleod_phoebe
f facebook.com/PhoebeMacleodAuthor
◎ instagram.com/phoebemacleod21

ALSO BY PHOEBE MACLEOD

Someone Else's Honeymoon

Not The Man I Thought He Was

Fred and Breakfast

Let's Not Be Friends

An (Un)Romantic Comedy

Love at First Site

Never Ever Getting Back Together

The Fixer Upper

My Not So Perfect Summer

Too Busy for Love

LOVE NOTES

LOVE IN EVERY CHAPTER

WHERE ALL YOUR ROMANCE
DREAMS COME TRUE!

THE HOME OF BESTSELLING
ROMANCE AND WOMEN'S
FICTION

 WARNING:
MAY CONTAIN SPICE

SIGN UP TO OUR
NEWSLETTER

https://bit.ly/Lovenotesnews

Boldwood

Boldwood Books is an award-winning fiction publishing company seeking out the best stories from around the world.

Find out more at www.boldwoodbooks.com

Join our reader community for brilliant books, competitions and offers!

Follow us

@BoldwoodBooks

@TheBoldBookClub

Sign up to our weekly deals newsletter

https://bit.ly/BoldwoodBNewsletter